D0388612

Foundations of
EMPOWERMENT
EVALUATION

This book is dedicated to my daughter,
Sarah Rachel Fetterman. A bright and beautiful
child with a joyful laugh, a good heart,
and a playful soul.

Foundations of
EMPOWERMENT EVALUATION

David M. Fetterman

Sage Publications, Inc.
International Educational and Professional Publisher
Thousand Oaks ■ London ■ New Delhi

Copyright 2001 by Sage Publications, Inc.

All rights reserved. No part of this book may be reproduced or utilized in any form or by any means, electronic or mechanical, including photocopying, recording, or by any information storage and retrieval system, without permission in writing from the publisher.

For information:

 Sage Publications, Inc.
2455 Teller Road
Thousand Oaks, California 91320
E-mail: order@sagepub.com

Sage Publications Ltd.
6 Bonhill Street
London EC2A 4PU
United Kingdom

Sage Publications India Pvt. Ltd.
M-32 Market
Greater Kailash I
New Delhi 110 048 India
Printed in the United States of America

Library of Congress Cataloging-in-Publication Data

This book is printed on acid-free paper.

Library of Congress Cataloging-in-Publication Data
Fetterman, David M.
    Foundations of empowerment evaluation / By David M. Fetterman.
        p.   cm.
Includes bibliographical references and index.
    ISBN 978-0-8039-5668-1 (cloth : alk. paper)
    ISBN 978-0-8039-5669-8 (pbk : alk. paper)
    1. Evaluation research (Social action programs) 2. Employee empowerment. 3. Human services—Evaluation. I. Title.
    H62 .F412 2000
    658.3'14—dc21
                                        00-009213

09 10 9 8 7 6 5

Acquiring Editor:	C. Deborah Laughton
Editorial Assistant:	Eileen Carr
Production Editor:	Astrid Virding
Editorial Assistant:	Cindy Bear
Designer/Typesetter:	Janelle LeMaster
Cover Designer:	Michelle Lee

CONTENTS

Never doubt that a small group of thoughtful,
committed people can change the world.
Indeed it is the only thIng that ever has.

—Margaret Mead

ACKNOWLEDGMENTS

How do you begin to thank an entire profession and association of colleagues and friends? The profession is as much a state of mind as it is an active force in the daily lives of evaluators, program staff members, program participants, and policy makers. It has created an environment conducive to the development of empowerment evaluation. Colleagues too numerous to mention throughout the world have conscientiously applied their insights, wisdom, and hard work to the task of translating knowledge into action. The list of acknowledgments, like the Internet, continues to unfold and expand every day. A few individuals of special note include the Empowerment Evaluation Institute partners, including Abraham Wandersman, Margret Dugan, and Andy Rowe. In addition, Shakeh Kaftarian from the Centers for Substance Abuse Prevention, has provided generous support and leadership in this area. The contributors of *Empowerment Evaluation: Knowledge and Tools for Self-Assessment and Accountability* (Fetterman, Kaftarian, & Wandersman, 1996) have also worked to build a solid foundation for empowerment evaluation in the field. A few of them include Henry Levin, Ricardo Millett, Joyce Keller, Cynthia Gomez and Ellen Goldstein, Cheryl Grills, Stephen Fawcett, Robert Yin, John Stevenson, Denis Mithaug, Jean Ann Linney, Frances Butterfoss, and Steven Mayer.

Michael Patton and Michael Scriven have provided insightful critiques of empowerment evaluation and in the process helped to refine and classify aspects of the approach. Daniel Stufflebeam provided the impetus to apply the standards to empowerment evaluation. Brad Cousins and his colleagues have contributed to greater conceptual clarity between collaborative, participatory, and empowerment evaluation. Jean King's leadership as co-chair of the Collaborative, Participatory, and Empowerment Evaluation topical interest group and her leadership along with Susan Kistler concerning the Minnesota Evaluation Studies Institute have enhanced discourse and understanding of empowerment evaluation. Lynn Usher's work remains an inspiration, particularly in terms of the scope of his self-evaluation efforts. Heather Weiss's work with the Harvard Family Research Project, and specifically The *Evaluation Exchange* has helped to disseminate knowledge about the development and use of collaborative, participatory, and empowerment evaluation-oriented approaches. Ernest House and Karen Kirkhart's emphasis on social justice in evaluation have influenced the shape and development of empowerment evaluation, as well. Will Shadish and Lee Sechrest have highlighted the global scope of this approach. Their observations are greatly appreciated particularly because, as past presidents of the American Evaluation Association, they have an insight into the type of effort required to successfully launch such an effort.

A special debt of gratitude is owed the Canadian Evaluation Society, who orchestrated a creative workshop/plenary exchange that helped clarify differences between empowerment evaluation, inclusive evaluation, and experimental design. Andy Rowe was principally responsible for the design of this conference, and Michael Patton was instrumental as a conference plenary facilitator.

Finally, my empowerment evaluation team members at Stanford University, some of whom are mentioned in this book, are responsible for facilitating projects throughout the world. They have remained rigorous, thoughtful, caring, and patient. Their contributions have come from the head and the heart. My debt to them is immeasurable.

INTRODUCTION

Introducing Empowerment Evaluation as a Part of the Intellectual Landscape of Evaluation

If I am not for myself, who will be for me? If I am only for myself, what am I? And if not now, when?

—Hillel

Empowerment evaluation is part of the intellectual landscape of evaluation. It has been adopted in higher education, government, inner-city public education, nonprofit corporations, and foundations throughout the United States and abroad. A wide range of program and policy sectors use empowerment evaluation, including substance abuse prevention, HIV prevention, crime prevention, environmental protection, welfare reform, battered women's shelters, agriculture and rural development, adult probation, adolescent pregnancy prevention, tribal partnership for substance

1

abuse, self-determination and individuals with disabilities, doctoral programs, and educational reform (e.g., the Accelerated Schools Project—a national educational reform movement). Descriptions of programs that use empowerment evaluation appear in *Empowerment Evaluation: Knowledge and Tools for Self-Assessment and Accountability* (Fetterman, Kaftarian, & Wandersman, 1996).This book provides additional insight into this evaluation approach. It presents a discussion about the background and theory of empowerment, and specifies the three steps of empowerment evaluation, as well as related facets. These steps are the most commonly used tools in workshops designed to train program staff members and participants to evaluate and improve their programs and practice (see Fetterman, 1994a, 1994b.) Chapter 4 highlights the steps with four case examples, ranging from hospital to educational settings. The utility, credibility, and rigor of empowerment evaluation are further documented in a high-stakes case example focusing on accreditation in higher education. This case example sets the stage for a discussion about empowerment evaluation and the standards in Chapter 6. Empowerment evaluation is consistent with the spirit of the standards developed by the Joint Committee on Standards for Educational Evaluation (1994; see also Fetterman, 1995), as well as the Guiding Principles for Evaluators (American Evaluation Association Task Force on Guiding Principles for Evaluators, 1995). It has also been institutionalized within the American Evaluation Association.[1] However, there are caveats and concerns that merit attention, and they are presented and confronted openly in Chapter 7. An attempt to distinguish empowerment evaluation from other approaches is found in Chapter 8, focusing on issues raised in the literature by prominent members of the association. These issues include process use; the relationship between collaborative, participatory, and empowerment evaluation; the target population; similarities with stakeholder and utilization-focused evaluation; advocacy; political correctness; accountability; consumer focus; movement; distance; internal and external evaluation; the use of an empowerment evaluator or consultant; and devolving responsibility. Chapter 8 also highlights a watershed moment in the literature on this topic focusing on Chelimsky's (1997) work in defining multiple purposes of evaluation, including development, accountability, and knowledge. This discussion allows evaluators to stop talking past each other or talking in terms of what is or is not evaluation. Instead, it redirects our attention to the more relevant discussion about when one approach is more useful or appropriate than another in practice. This book concludes with a discussion about the role of the Internet in disseminating empowerment evaluation and the strengths, weaknesses, and conditions of empowerment evaluation. A brief introduction to empowerment evaluation is presented below to set the stage for this far ranging exploration into this approach.

■ An Overview

Empowerment evaluation is the use of evaluation concepts, techniques, and findings to foster improvement and self-determination. It employs both qualitative and quantitative methodologies. Although it can be applied to individuals, organizations,[2] communities, and societies or cultures, the focus is usually on programs. Empowerment evaluation has an unambiguous value orientation: It is designed to help people help themselves and improve their programs using a form of self-evaluation and reflection. Program participants—including clients—conduct their own evaluations; an outside evaluator often serves as a coach or additional facilitator depending on internal program capabilities. Empowerment evaluation is necessarily a collaborative activity, not an individual pursuit. An evaluator does not and cannot empower anyone; people empower themselves, often with assistance and coaching. Empowerment evaluation can create an environment that is conducive to empowerment and self-determination. This process is fundamentally democratic in the sense that it invites (if not demands) participation, examining issues of concern to the entire community in an open forum. As a result, the context changes: the assessment of a program's value and worth is not the endpoint of the evaluation—as it often is in traditional evaluation—but is part of an ongoing process of program improvement. This new context acknowledges a simple but often overlooked truth: merit and worth are not static values. Populations shift, goals shift, knowledge about program practices and their value change, and external forces are highly unstable. By internalizing and institutionalizing self-evaluation processes and practices, a dynamic and responsive approach to evaluation can be developed to accommodate these shifts. As Usher (1995) explains,

> By developing the capacity to monitor and assess their own performance, program managers and staff can risk the mistakes that often occur with innovation. This is because they can detect problems and make midcourse corrections before the results of errors due to planning *or* execution become widely

apparent and costly. Having the capacity *and* responsibility to obtain such information about program operations and impact thus empowers managers
and staff to explore new ways to enhance their performance. (pp. 62–63)

Both value assessments and corresponding plans for program improvement—developed by the group with the assistance of a trained evaluator—
are subject to a cyclical process of reflection and self-evaluation. Program
participants learn continually to assess their progress toward self-
determined goals and to reshape their plans and strategies according to
this assessment. In the process, self-determination is fostered, illumination generated, and liberation actualized.Value assessments are also
highly sensitive to the life cycle of the program or organization. Goals and
outcomes are geared toward the appropriate developmental level of implementation. Extraordinary improvements are not expected of a project
that will not be fully implemented until the following year. Similarly,
seemingly small gains or improvements in programs at an embryonic
stage are recognized and appreciated in relation to their stage of development. In a fully operational and mature program, moderate improvements or declining outcomes are viewed more critically.

■ Pursuit of Truth and Honesty

Empowerment evaluation is guided by many principles. One of the most
important is a commitment to truth and honesty. This is not a naive concept of one absolute truth, but a sincere intent to understand an event in
context and from multiple worldviews. The aim is to try to understand a
situation from the participant's own perspective as accurately and honestly as possible, and then to proceed to improve it with meaningful goals
and strategies and with credible documentation. As in traditional evaluation, empowerment evaluation findings are based on data, including
harsh criticism of program performance as well as information about program strengths. An important difference, however, is that the stakeholders—program staff members and participants, in concert with
funders and other external agencies—establish their own goals, processes,
outcomes, and impacts. In addition, the program staff members and participants conduct a self-evaluation, usually with training, coaching, and
assistance from external empowerment evaluators.Empowerment evalu-

ation is conducted with a strong, shared commitment to "speaking your truth"; deception is inappropriate, and the group proves a useful and powerful check on any attempt to sugarcoat the findings. There are many checks and balances in empowerment evaluation, such as having a democratic approach to participation—involving participants at all levels of the organization; relying on external evaluators as critical friends; and so on. Empowerment evaluation is like a personnel performance self-appraisal. An employee comes to an agreement with his or her supervisor about their goals, strategies for accomplishing those goals, and credible documentation to determine if the employee is meeting these goals. The employee then makes the same agreement with his or her clients. If the data are not credible, the employee loses credibility immediately; if, however, the data are credible and merit it, employees can, at the end of the year, use the data to advocate for themselves. Empowerment evaluation applies the same approach to the program and community level. Advocacy, in this context, becomes a natural byproduct of the self-evaluation process—if the data merit it. Advocacy is meaningless in the absence of credible data. In addition, external standards and/or requirements can significantly influence any self-evaluation. To operate without consideration of these external forces is to proceed at your own peril. However, the process must be grounded in an authentic understanding and expression of everyday life at the program or community level. A commitment to the ideals of truth and honesty guides every step and facet of empowerment evaluation.

■ Steps of Empowerment Evaluation

Empowerment evaluation has three steps. The first step is establishing a mission or vision statement about the program. Some groups do not like the terms *mission* or *vision,* and instead prefer to focus on results. They state the results they would like to see based on the outcome of the implemented program, and map backwards—specifying activities required to achieve those processes and outcomes. The second step, taking stock, involves identifying and prioritizing the most significant program activities. Then, program staff members and participants rate how well the program is doing in each of those activities, typically on a 1 (*low*) to 10 (*high*) scale, and discuss the ratings. This helps to determine where the program stands, including current strengths and weaknesses. The third step involves charting a course for the future. The group states goals and strategies to achieve their dreams. Goals help program staff members and participants determine where they want to go in the future with an explicit emphasis on program improvement. Strategies help them accomplish program goals. These efforts are monitored using credible documentation. Empowerment evaluators help program staff members and participants identify the type of evidence required to document progress toward their goals. Evaluation becomes a part of the normal planning and management of the program, which is a means of institutionalizing and internalizing evaluation.

■ Facets of Empowerment Evaluation

In this new context, training, facilitation, advocacy, illumination, and liberation are all facets—if not developmental stages—of empowerment evaluation. Rather than additional roles for an evaluator, whose primary function is to assess worth (as defined by Scriven, 1967, and Stufflebeam, 1994), these facets are an integral part of the evaluation process. Cronbach's (1980) developmental focus is relevant: The emphasis is on program development, improvement, and lifelong learning.

■ Dynamic Community of Learners

Many elements must be in place for empowerment evaluation to be effective and credible. Participants must have the latitude to experiment, taking both risks and responsibility for their actions. An environment conducive to sharing successes and failures is also essential. In addition, an honest, self-critical, trusting, and supportive atmosphere is required. As Anthony J. D'Angelo observes, "Without a sense of caring, there can be no sense of community." Conditions need not be perfect to initiate this process; however, the accuracy and usefulness of self-ratings improve dramatically in this context. An outside evaluator charged with monitoring the process can help keep the effort credible, useful, and on track, providing additional rigor, reality checks, and quality controls throughout the evaluation. Without any of these elements in place, the exercise may be self-serving and of limited utility; with many of these elements in place, the exercise can create a dynamic community of transformative learning (see Argyris & Schon, 1978; Mezirow, 1978).

■ Conclusion

Empowerment evaluation is fundamentally a democratic process. The entire group—not a single individual, not the external evaluator or an internal manager—is responsible for conducting the evaluation. The group thus can serve as a check on its own members, moderating the various biases and agendas of individual participants. The evaluator is a co-equal in this endeavor, not a superior and not a servant; as a critical friend, the evaluator can question shared biases or "group think." As is the case in traditional evaluation, everyone is accountable in one fashion or another, and thus has an interest or agenda to protect. A school district may have a 5-year plan designed by the superintendent; a graduate school may have to satisfy requirements of an accreditation association; an outside evaluator may have an important but demanding sponsor pushing either timelines or results, or may be influenced by training to use one theoretical approach rather than another. Empowerment evaluations, like all other evaluations, exist within a context. However, the range of macrogoals and intermediate objectives linking what most people do in their daily routine is almost infinite. People often feel empowered and self-determined when they can select intermediate objectives that are linked to larger, global goals. In addition, a self-evaluation is more meaningful when linked to external requirements and demands. Empowerment evaluation also empowers external evaluators. Specifically, the external evaluator's role and productivity is enhanced by the presence of an empowerment or internal evaluation process. Most evaluators operate significantly below their capacity in an evaluation because the program lacks even rudimentary evaluation mechanisms and processes. The external evaluator routinely devotes time to the development and maintenance of elementary evaluation systems. Programs that already have a basic self-evaluation process in place enable external evaluators to begin operating at a much more sophisticated level. Finally, as Vanderplaat (1997) explains,

> Perhaps what distinguishes the discourse on empowerment most clearly from its predecessors is its acknowledgement and deep respect for people's

capacity to create knowledge about, and solutions to, their own experiences. (p. 147)

A brief discussion about the historical roots, influences, theory, and case examples is offered in the next chapter to help illuminate many of the forces driving empowerment evaluation.

■ Notes

1.   Empowerment evaluation has been institutionalized as part of the Collaborative, Participatory, and Empowerment Evaluation Topical Interest Group (TIG) of the American Evaluation Association. TIG chairs are David Fetterman and Jean King.

2.   See Stevenson, Mitchell, and Florin (1996) for a detailed explanation about the distinctions concerning levels of organizations. See also Zimmerman (in press) for more detail about empowerment theory focusing on psychological, organizational, and community levels of analysis.

2

BACKGROUND AND THEORY

Exploring the Background and Theory of Empowerment Evaluation With Relevant Examples and Tools

What's past is prologue.

—*William Shakespeare*

Empowerment evaluation served as the theme for the 1993 American Evaluation Association annual meeting as well as the basis for my presidential address (Fetterman, 1994a). The topic stimulated conversations and arguments that spilled out into the hallways during the conference. It was a timely approach, reflecting the interests, needs, and practices of a significant number of evaluators. The dialogue that empowerment evaluation initiated at the meeting spilled over into the journals, stimulating intense discussion in *Evaluation Practice* in particular. This high level of intellectual and emotional engagement—both positive and negative—

suggests that this approach speaks to issues at the very heart of the evaluation community. It acknowledges the significance of this approach as a contribution in its own right and as a tool in helping us refine and redefine evaluation use.

■ Background

Empowerment evaluation has many sources. The idea first germinated for me during preparation of another book, *Speaking the language of power: Communication, collaboration, and advocacy* (Fetterman, 1993b). In developing that collection, I wanted to explore the many ways that evaluators and social scientists could give voice to the people they work with and bring their concerns to policybrokers. I found that, increasingly, socially concerned scholars in myriad fields are making their insights and findings available to decision makers. These scholars and practitioners address a host of significant issues, including conflict resolution, the dropout problem, environmental health and safety, homelessness, educational reform, AIDS, American Indian concerns, and the education of gifted children. The aim of these scholars and practitioners was to explore successful strategies, share lessons learned, and enhance their ability to communicate with an educated citizenry and powerful policy-making bodies. Collaboration, participation, and empowerment emerged as common threads throughout the work, and helped to crystallize the concept of empowerment evaluation.

Empowerment evaluation has roots in community psychology, action anthropology, and action research. Community psychology focuses on people, organizations, and communities working to establish control over their affairs. The literature about citizen participation and community development is extensive. Rappaport's "Terms of empowerment/Exemplars of prevention: Toward a theory for community psychology" (1987) is a classic in this area. Sol Tax's (1958) work in action anthropology focuses on how anthropologists can facilitate the goals and objectives of self-determining groups, such as Native American tribes. Empowerment evaluation also derives from collaborative and participatory evaluation (see Choudhary & Tandon, 1988; Oja & Smulyan, 1989; Papineau & Kiely, 1994; Reason, 1988; Shapiro, 1988; Stull & Schensul, 1987; Whitmore, 1991; Whyte, 1990).

■ Influences

Empowerment evaluation has influenced and been strongly influenced by action research. Stakeholders typically control the study and conduct the work in action research and empowerment evaluation. In addition, practitioners empower themselves in both forms of inquiry and action. Empowerment evaluation and action research are characterized by concrete, timely, targeted, pragmatic orientations toward program improvement. They both require cycles of reflection and action, and focus on the simplest data collection methods adequate to the task at hand. However, there are conceptual and stylistic differences between the approaches. For example, empowerment evaluation is explicitly driven by the concept of self-determination. It is also explicitly collaborative in nature. Action research, on the other hand, can be either an individual effort documented in a journal or a group effort, with written narratives used to share findings with colleagues (see Soffer, 1995). A group collaboratively conducts empowerment evaluation, with a holistic focus on an entire program or agency: Empowerment evaluation is never conducted by a single individual. Action research is often conducted in addition to the normal daily responsibilities of a practitioner, whereas empowerment evaluation is internalized as part of the planning and management of a program. The institutionalization of evaluation, in this manner, makes it more likely to be sustainable rather than sporadic. In spite of these differences, the overwhelming number of similarities between the approaches has enriched empowerment evaluation.

Another major influence on the development of empowerment evaluation was one of the national educational school reform movements by colleagues such as Henry Levin, whose Accelerated School Project (ASP) emphasizes the empowerment of parents, teachers, and administrators to improve educational settings. We worked to help design an appropriate evaluation plan for the Accelerated School Project that contributes to the empowerment of teachers, parents, students, and administrators (Fetterman & Haertel, 1990). The ASP team and I also mapped out detailed strategies for districtwide adoption of the project in an effort to help institutionalize the project in the school system (Stanford University and American Institutes for Research, 1992).

A pragmatic influence on empowerment evaluation is the W. K. Kellogg Foundation's emphasis on empowerment in community settings. The foundation has taken a clear position concerning empowerment as a funding strategy:

> We've long been convinced that problems can best be solved at the local level by people who live with them on a daily basis. In other words, individuals and groups of people must be empowered to become change makers and solve their own problems, through the organizations and institutions they devise. ... Through our community-based programming, we are helping to empower various individuals, agencies, institutions, and organizations to work together to identify problems and to find quality, cost-effective solutions. In doing so, we find ourselves working more than ever with grantees with whom we have been less involved—smaller, newer organizations and their programs. (W. K. Kellogg Foundation, 1992, p. 6)

Kellogg's work in the areas of youth, leadership, community-based health services, higher education, food systems, rural development, and families and neighborhoods exemplifies this spirit of putting "power in the hands of creative and committed individuals—power that will enable them to make important changes in the world" (p. 13). For example, one project, Kellogg's Empowering Farm Women to Reduce Hazards to Family Health and Safety on the Farm, involves a participatory evaluation component. The work of Sanders, Barley, and Jenness (1990) on cluster evaluations for the Kellogg Foundation also highlights the value of giving ownership of the evaluation to project directors and staff members of science education projects.

■ Theory

Dennis Mithaug's (1991, 1993) extensive work with individuals with disabilities to explore concepts of self-regulation and self-determination provided additional inspiration. Dennis and I, as part of an American Institutes for Research team, completed a 2-year Department of Education–funded grant on self-determination and individuals with disabilities. We conducted research designed to help both providers for students with disabilities and the students themselves become more empowered. We learned about self-determined behavior and attitudes and environmentally related features of self-determination by listening to self-determined children with disabilities and their providers. Using specific concepts and behaviors extracted from these case studies, we developed a behavioral checklist to assist providers as they work to recognize and foster self-determination.

Self-determination, defined as the ability to chart one's own course in life, forms the theoretical foundation of empowerment evaluation. It consists of numerous interconnected capabilities, such as the ability to identify and express needs; to establish goals or expectations and a plan of action to achieve them; to identify resources; to make rational choices from various alternative courses of action; to take appropriate steps to pursue objectives; to evaluate short- and long-term results, including reassessing plans and expectations and taking necessary detours; and to persist in the pursuit of those goals. A breakdown at any juncture of this network of capabilities—as well as various environmental factors—can reduce a person's likelihood of being self-determined. (Concerning the self-efficacy mechanism in human agency, see Bandura, 1982.)

Zimmerman's work on empowerment theory provides an additional theoretical framework for empowerment evaluation, focusing on processes and outcomes. According to Zimmerman (in press),

A distinction between empowering processes and outcomes is critical in order to clearly define empowerment theory. Empowerment processes are ones in which attempts to gain control, obtain needed resources, and critically understand one's social environment are fundamental. The process is empowering if it helps people develop skills so they can become independent problem solvers and decision makers. Empowering processes will vary across levels of analysis. For example, empowering processes for individuals might include organizational or community involvement, empowering processes at the organizational level might include shared leadership and decision making, and empowering processes at the community level might include accessible government, media, and other community resources.

Empowered outcomes refer to operationalization of empowerment so we can study the consequences of citizen attempts to gain greater control in their community or the effects of interventions designed to empower participants. Empowered outcomes also differ across levels of analysis. When we are concerned with individuals, outcomes might include situation-specific perceived control, skills, and proactive behaviors. When we are studying organizations, outcomes might include organizational networks, effective resource acquisition, and policy leverage. When we are concerned with community level empowerment, outcomes might include evidence of pluralism, the existence of organizational coalitions, and accessible community resources.

■ Role

Zimmerman's (in press) characterization of the community psychologist's role in empowering activities is easily adapted to the empowerment evaluator:

> An empowerment approach to intervention design, implementation, and evaluation redefines the professional's role relationship with the target population. The professional's role becomes one of collaborator and facilitator rather than expert and counselor. As collaborators, professionals learn about the participants through their culture, their worldview, and their life struggles. The professional works *with* participants instead of advocating *for* them. The professional's skills, interest, or plans are not imposed on the community; rather, professionals become a resource for a community. This role relationship suggests that what professionals do will depend on the particular place and people with whom they are working, rather than on the technologies that are predetermined to be applied in all situations. While interpersonal assessment and evaluation skills will be necessary, how, where, and with whom they are applied can not be automatically assumed as in the role of a psychotherapist with clients in a clinic.

An eloquent literature on empowerment theory by Zimmerman (in press), Zimmerman, Israel, Schulz, and Checkoway (1992), Zimmerman and Rappaport (1988), and Dunst, Trivette, and LaPointe (1992) also informs this approach. The evolving nature of empowerment evaluation as it is applied in practice merits some discussion, as it shapes and informs future practice.

■ Examples

Empowerment evaluations vary in size and scope. However, they are all shaped by a focus on self-determination, capacity building, and helping others evaluate themselves. The Accelerated Schools Project (ASP) is part of the national educational reform movement in the United States, encompassing more than 700 elementary and middle schools in 37 states. ASP embodies the concept of empowerment evaluation: fostering self-determination and ongoing program improvement. ASP staff members provide training to build capacity and serve as coaches (rather than experts) to work with schools. Members of the school community are involved in the process of taking stock through systematic inquiry, which includes identifying significant issues and activities, developing evaluative questions, collecting and analyzing data, and reporting findings. Baseline data from this process are compared with the school's vision. Differences between the baseline and the vision are prioritized, and form the basis of plans for the future. Members of the school community develop criteria to determine whether they are approximating their goals, including specific observable outcomes. Moreover, ASP is a reflective, self-evaluating entity by its nature, examining its fidelity to the process and to self-determined goals in its quest for continuous improvement. (See Levin, 1996.)

The W. K. Kellogg Foundation is one of the largest foundations in the world, with expenditures exceeding $260 million per year. The foundation's approach to program evaluation from its earliest conception was designed to help others help themselves. Evaluation at the foundation is considered part of programming rather than a separate function, as a tool for organizational learning, a developmental ongoing process (not a single summative report card), and a collaborative relationship between grant-maker and grant-seeker. Empowerment evaluation at the Kellogg Foundation is designed to "improve, not prove" (Millett, 1996, p. 69). The foundation places evaluation responsibility in the hands of grantees with the aim of institutionalizing evaluation within each organization. This view is more fully elaborated in the W. K. Kellogg Foundation publication "Empowerment Evaluation and Foundations: A Matter of Perspectives" (1999; see also Millett, 1996).

Another example is the Marin Community Foundation in California, which is one of the most well-endowed foundations in the country. Their California Health Access Provider (CHAP) project was designed to improve access to health care for indigent and disenfranchised populations. The Foundation was successful in bringing over seven separate, and often competing, agencies together in this effort. They had a two-part action plan that resulted in the creation of an environment that facilitated collaboration and self-determination. First, they provided funding requiring cooperation among health service providers, instead of the traditional competitive model in which separate health service agencies compete for the same scarce dollars. Second, they introduced empowerment evaluation as a tool to foster self-determination and collaboration among health service providers, requiring group planning, implementation, and evaluation. I provided initial matrix model workshops (discussed in Chapter 4) and Margret Dugan provided guidance and instruction throughout the evaluation, highlighting the use of logic models to map out strategies and objectives. The community-based CHAP empowerment evaluation team has become so enthusiastic about the effectiveness of empowerment evaluation they have presented their efforts at various professional association meetings.

The Mary Black Foundation has also used empowerment evaluation to improve grantmaking. They require a partnership between the funder, grantee, and evaluator. Those applying to the foundation use empowerment evaluation to write better proposals. In addition, empowerment evaluation tools help to establish a common set of accountability standards and outcomes, improving the probability of program success and improvement. (See Wandersman, Imm, Crusto, & Andra, 1999; Yost 1998.)

The Center for Substance Abuse Prevention (CSAP) community partnerships programs provide another excellent example of the use of empowerment evaluation to build capacity and improve programs throughout the country. CSAP has taken the lead in a collaborative model that requires local-level self-evaluations designed to improve problem solving and program practice in more than 250 comprehensive community programs. Technical assistance and training are conducted within the context of an ongoing evaluative process, not as ends in themselves. (See Yin, Kaftarian, & Jacobs, 1996.)

Colleges have adopted empowerment evaluation to institutionalize evaluation and facilitate accreditation self-studies and strategic planning. Cambridge College in Massachusetts is conducting an extensive long-term empowerment evaluation designed to track student pathways and demographics, document student learning outcomes, and record impacts on students' lives outside the college (alumni data). In addition, they have used empowerment evaluation concepts and tools to describe and explore formal contexts for learning in the college, including classrooms, colloquia, community meetings, and practica/internships. The entire process of designing and implementing institutional research has been collaborative, participatory, and empowering.[1] (See Moreton & Pursley, 1998.)

State government agencies have used empowerment evaluation highlighting various stages of the process, including taking stock and planning for the future. (See Keller, 1996.) State agencies often introduce empowerment evaluation after a traditional approach fails, recognizing their clients want to be a part of the process. Evaluators in this context are facilitators, advocates, trainers, coaches, mentors, and occasionally experts. They provide useful evaluation frameworks and logic models to facilitate the process and to identify stages, participants' tasks, evaluators' tasks, and evaluators' roles. Program participants typically provide an objective, often brutally self-critical, analytical review of their programs in these efforts (see Dugan, 1996).

HIV Prevention programs have adopted empowerment evaluation concepts and techniques to forge collaborative working relationships between service providers, academics, and private funders in the fight against AIDS—the leading cause of death for adults aged 22 to 45 in the United States. This approach is used to empower rather than to judge, to share skills and knowledge rather than to find fault, and to improve program practice. Evaluators facilitate rather than implement the evaluation effort. Workshops are designed for capacity building—helping community-based organizations learn how to write proposals for support and to evaluate their own services. (See Gomez & Goldstein, 1996.)

African American communities with a tradition of self-determination have adopted empowerment evaluation for community organizing, public policy work, and planning and prevention strategies for substance abuse prevention and treatment. Civil rights and community activists constantly debrief, critique, evaluate, and refine their work to address economic problems that contribute to cocaine trafficking, educational inequalities that result in unemployment, and the proliferation of liquor stores that contribute to a host of destructive and often violent behaviors. The values of empowerment evaluation are consistent with community activism, and the evaluation rigor enhanced and refined an existing self-reflective cultural practice within the community coalition. (See Grills, Bass, Brown, & Akers, 1996.)

Empowerment evaluation has been useful in helping United Way-affiliated battered women's emergency shelters and Habitat for Humanity pursue their goals. Empowerment evaluation was adopted because it was consistent with the ideals of the service organizations, responsive to and dependent on the wisdom of program participants, and focused on program improvement and accountability (see Andrews, 1996.) Community coalitions have also found empowerment evaluation helpful, particularly in the areas of adolescent pregnancy prevention, adolescent and adult substance abuse, and tribal substance abuse prevention. In these efforts, the aim has been to legitimize community members' experiential knowledge, acknowledge the role of values in research and evaluation, empower community members, democratize research inquiry, and enhance the relevance of evaluation data for communities. Work in this area has highlighted the multiple goals of empowerment evaluation, which involve self-assessment of merit as a tool to foster improvement and self-determination at every stage. (See Fawcett, Paine-Andrews, Francisco, Schultz, Richter, Lewis, Harris, Williams, Berkley, Lopez, & Fisher, 1996.)

Other community coalitions focusing on the reduction of alcohol and other drug abuse recognize the critical role evaluators play in building the learning capacity of organizations as part of the evaluation process—fundamental aspects of empowerment evaluation practice (see Stevenson, Mitchell, & Florin, 1996.) A few additional examples are listed below to further provide a sense of the scope and range of organizations using empowerment evaluation. For example, the teachers of the Nueva School (a progressive school for gifted and talented students in California) have adopted empowerment evaluation to refine the art of teaching in a sustainable environment. This group exemplifies the spirit of empowerment evaluation in many ways, including taking the initiative to pursue goals on their own. The Nueva teachers decided to conduct their own workshop, in between one of the scheduled series of coach-facilitated workshops, and reprioritized their concerns without the evaluation coaches. When the evaluation team returned, the Nueva teachers presented us with the new set of goals that they wanted to pursue with our facilitation assistance.

The Youth Empowerment Evaluation Initiative, facilitated by Community LORE, a San Francisco–based nonprofit consulting and training firm committed to social justice and youth development, demonstrates how youth conduct their own program evaluations (Zimmerman & Erbstein, 1999).[2] The U.S. Department of Agriculture's Community Food Projects (a food security initiative), as well as the Environmental Protection Agency's efforts highlight federal involvement with and use of empowerment evaluation. Additional projects are reported on the Collaborative, Participatory, and Empowerment Evaluation web page at <http://www.stanford.edu/~davidf/empowermentevaluation.html>.

■ Tools

A long list of tools and techniques has emerged from empowerment and self-evaluations. For example, the *Program Evaluation Tool Kit: A Blueprint for Public Health Management* (Porteous, Sheldrick, & Stewart, 1997) is an excellent guide designed to integrate evaluation into the management of programs. *Everyday Evaluation on the Run* (Wadsworth, 1997) provides a highly user-friendly guide to self-evaluation. The Prevention Plus III Model (Linney & Wandersman, 1996) is a public domain four-step approach to assessing school and community prevention programs designed as an evaluation tool for use by nonprofessionals. *Focusing on Program Outcomes: A Guide for United Ways* (United Way, 1996a) and *Measuring Program Outcomes: A Practical Approach* (United Way, 1996b) are outcome evaluation guides developed by United Way of America. The *Community Self-Evaluation Workbook* (1995) was produced by the U.S. Department of Justice's Office of Juvenile Justice and Delinquency Prevention, and the U.S. Department of Education publishes *Making Information Work for You* (1997).

The plan quality index is a research tool to assess the quality of community plans. It is also used to structure feedback to coalition staff members and participants to help them improve their community-based prevention plans and activities (Butterfoss, Goodman, Wandersman, Valois, & Chinman, 1996). The empowerment evaluation matrix is a spreadsheet designed to facilitate the prioritization and rating or assessment of program activities. It also is used to facilitate dialogue about staff member and participant ratings concerning program activities (Fetterman, 1998a). Logic models are used to help program participants make the theory of their program explicit. Basically, logic models are used to help staff members and participants explain how their program works, which provides a benchmark to measure against and increases their confidence in their own ability to describe and measure what they do (Dugan, 1996).

In addition, women's empowerment logs help mothers notice and record their daily efforts to overcome barriers to greater self-sufficiency as they try to get off welfare. An affordable housing evaluation toolbox provides residents with ready-to-administer surveys, instructions for conducting focus groups, and sample report outlines for reporting outcomes. The toolbox is designed to help residents strengthen their quality of life in affordable housing developments. A book concerning leadership programs for community foundations provides insights into codiscovered lessons on the dynamics of growth. A crime and drug prevention assessment, in which Mayer (1996) participated, provided a model "prevention forum" designed to create local ownership of the evaluations, build and strengthen links among different kinds of community participants, and help community members build their own local critical abilities on crime and drug abuse.

A few include self-help evaluation tools on the web to facilitate empowerment evaluation. There are the *W. K. Kellogg Foundation Evaluation Handbook* at <http://www.wkkf.org/Publications/evalhdbk/default.htm>; the National Science Foundation's *User-friendly handbook for mixed method evaluations* at <http://www.nsf.gov/cgi-bin/getpub?nsf97153> and their *User-friendly handbook for project evaluation* at <http://www.ehr.nsf.gov/ EHR/RED/EVAL/handbook/handbook.htm>; and the Bureau of Justice's Evaluation Web Site at <http://www.bja.evaluationwebsite.org/html/ roadmap/index.html>. The Annie E. Casey Foundation tools developed through the Family-to-Family initiative—including the tool developed by Lynn Usher's group in Chapel Hill, *The need for self-evaluation: Using data to guide policy and practice*—are available at <http://www.aecf.org/familyto-family/tools.htm>.

SRI's Directorate for Education and Human Resources has also made a web-based resource available to conduct evaluations at <http:// oerl.sri.com/>. Materials include evaluation plans, instruments, and reports; guidelines; criteria for judging quality; and glossaries elaborating criteria. Project categories include curriculum development, teacher education, faculty development, laboratory improvement, and underrepresented populations.

InnoNet, a nonprofit organization that provides participatory evaluation services to other nonprofits, has provided an evaluation toolbox on the web at <http://www.innonet.org>. *CDC EZ-Text,* a free Windows software program, is a qualitative program developed to assist researchers in creating, managing, and analyzing semistructured qualitative databases.[3] The URL for this program is <http://www.cdc.gov/nchstp/hiv_aids/software/ez-text.htm>. Similarly, *AnSWR* (Analysis Software for Word-Based Records) is another free Windows software system for coordinating and conducting large-scale, team-based analysis projects that integrate qualitative and quantitative techniques.[4] The URL for that system is <http:// www.cdc.gov/nchstp/hiv_aids/software/answr.htm>. There are also various commercial software programs that facilitate empowerment evaluations, including *PROMES2*, which stands for Project Management, Monitoring, and Evaluation System. *PROMES2* can be used for a traditional or participatory process.[5]

The work of Kretzmann, McKnight, and Sheehan has been useful to guide community-based evaluations. You can order Kretzmann, McKnight, and Sheehan's *Guide to Capacity Inventories: Mobilizing the Community Skills of Local Residents* (1997) at <http://www.nwu.edu/IPR/publications/capinv.html>, and download Kretzmann and McKnight's *Mapping Community Capacity* (1990) from <http://www.nwu.edu/IPR/publications/mcc.html>. The Asset-Based Community Development Institute at Northwestern University also has a useful site at <http://www.nwu.edu/urban-affairs/programs/abcd.html>.

Paul Jahnige's organization, Community Resources,[6] completed the pilot development of an urban participatory community assessment method called "Knowing your community showing your community." It is a useful tool for participatory and empowerment evaluation efforts with urban and disadvantaged communities. Their URL is <http://www.community-resources.org/pua.htm>. Finally, the *Program evaluation tool kit: A blueprint for public health management* (Porteous, Sheldrick, & Stewart, 1997), described above, is at <http://www.uottawa.ca/academic/med/epid/toolkit.htm>.

This brief review of successful efforts provides an insight into the range and scope of empowerment evaluations. In addition, each reported empowerment evaluation project has served to refine the process and helped to identify the optimal conditions for, as well as the limitations of, the approach. Many projects have developed useful tools to facilitate the process. This discussion highlights the historical roots, influences, theory, and case examples that form the background for this evaluation approach, and also provides the foundation and rationale for many of the steps and facets of empowerment evaluation discussed in the next chapter.

■ Notes

1. Margret Dugan and I serve as advisory panel members on this project. In this case, we represent evaluation consultants rather than empowerment evaluators.

2. Elizabeth Whitmore at the Carleton University's School of Social Work in Ottawa, Canada, is currently doing interesting work in this area. Youth there are conducting their own evaluations, including writing their own reports.

3. Researchers can design a series of data entry templates tailored to their questionnaire. These questionnaires are usually administered during face-to-face interviews with a sample of respondents. A response to a question may be entered into *EZ-Text* either as a verbatim transcript (e.g., from a tape recording), or a summary generated from the interviewer's notes. Data from respondents can be typed directly into the templates or copied from word processor documents. Following data entry, investigators can interactively create on-line codebooks, apply codes to specific response passages, develop case studies, conduct database searches to identify text passages that meet user-specified conditions, and export data in a wide array of formats for further analysis with other qualitative or statistical analysis software programs. Project managers can merge data files generated by different interviewers for combined cross-site analyses. The ability to export and import the codebook helps to coordinate the efforts of multiple coders simultaneously working with copies of the same database file.

4. *AnSWR* has been designed to meet the following qualitative data analysis needs: coordination of team-based qualitative data analysis; management of large, complex qualitative data bases; fully integrated quantitative data components; structured codebook development; hierarchical coding structures; text coding; intercoder agreement assessments, including kappa; flexible reporting options with multiple boolean selection criteria (e.g., files, codes, coders, and quantitative variables); and output formats that facilitate import into both quantitative and qualitative programs.

5. The contact information for *PROMES2* is as follows: mailing address: Management for Development Foundation, Attention: Ms. Annet van Lier, P.O. Box 430, 6710 BK Ede, The Netherlands; telephone: (+31) 318 650060;

e-mail: mdf@mdf.nld.toolnet.org.

6. Community Resources can be contacted at the following: mailing address: Paul Jahnige, Community Resources, 5131 Wetheredsville Road, Baltimore, MD 21207; telephone: (410) 448-0640; fax: (410) 448-0874;

e-mail: director@ communityresources.org.

The group's web site can be accessed at <http://www.communityresources.org>.

THREE STEPS

Presenting the Three Steps of Empowerment Evaluation and Related Facets

Everything should be made as simple as possible, but not simpler.

—Albert Einstein

■ Steps of Empowerment Evaluation

There are three steps involved in helping others learn to evaluate their own programs: (a) developing a mission, vision, or unifying purpose; (b) taking stock or determining where the program stands, including strengths and weaknesses; and (c) planning for the future by establishing goals and helping participants determine their own strategies to accomplish program goals and objectives. In addition, empowerment evaluators help program staff members and participants determine the type of evidence required to document and monitor credibly the progress toward their goals. These steps combined help to create a "communicative space" (Vanderplaat, 1995) to facilitate emancipatory and "communicative action" (Habermas, 1984).

Mission

The first step in an empowerment evaluation is to ask program staff members and participants to define their mission. This step can be accomplished in a few hours. An empowerment evaluator facilitates an open session with as many staff members and participants as possible.

Participants are asked to generate key phrases that capture the mission of the program or project. This is done even when an existing mission statement exists, because there are typically many new participants and the initial document may or may not have been generated in a democratic, open forum. Proceeding in this fashion allows fresh new ideas to become a part of the mission, and also allows participants an opportunity to voice their vision of the program. It is common for groups to learn how divergent their participants' views are about the program, even when they have been working together for years. The evaluator records these phrases, typically on a poster sheet.

Then a workshop participant is asked to volunteer to write these telescopic phrases into a paragraph or two. This document is shared with the group, revisions and corrections are made in the process, and then the group is asked to accept the document on a consensus basis: that is, they do not have to be in favor of 100% of the document; they just have to be willing to live with it. The mission statement represents the values of the group and, as such, represents the foundation for the next step, taking stock.

Taking Stock

The second step in an empowerment evaluation is taking stock. This step can also be conducted in a few hours, and has two sections. The first involves generating a list of current key activities crucial to the functioning of the program. Once again, the empowerment evaluator serves as a facilitator, asking program staff members and participants to list the most significant features and/or activities associated with the program. A list of 10 to 20 activities is sufficient. After generating this list, it is time to prioritize

Figure 3.1. This is a picture of David Fetterman serving as an empowerment evaluation facilitator. The group provides the ideas and the information while he records it on the poster paper. He is responsible for making sure everyone is given an opportunity to speak, and he serves as a critical friend—challenging them to clarify terms, ideas, and judgments.

and determine which are the most important activities meriting evaluation at this time.

One tool used to minimize the time associated with prioritizing activities involves voting with dots. The empowerment evaluator gives each participant five dot stickers, and asks the participants to place them by the activity on which the participant wants to focus. The participant can distribute them across five different activities or place all five on one activity. Counting the dots easily identifies the top 10 activities. The 10 activities with the most dots become the prioritized list of activities meriting evaluation at that time. (This process avoids long arguments about why one activity is valued more than another is, when both activities are included in the list of the top ten program activities anyway.)

The second phase of taking stock involves rating the activities. Program staff members and participants are asked to rate how well they are doing concerning each activity on a 1 to 10 scale, with 10 as the highest level and 1 as the lowest. The staff members and participants only have minimal definitions about the components or activities at this point. Additional clarification can be pursued as needed; however, detailed definition and clarification become a significant part of the later dialogue process. (The group will never reach the rating stage if each activity is perfectly defined at this point. The rating process then sets the stage for dialogue, clarification, and communication.)

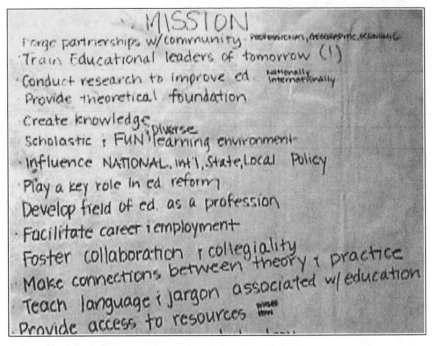

Figure 3.2. This poster documents the first phase in developing a School of Education mission statement. The facilitator records program participant phrases concerning the mission on this poster sheet. Later, these phrases are transformed into a more formal document, ranging in length from a paragraph to a couple of pages.

Typically, participants rate each of the activities while in their seats on their own piece of paper. Then they are asked to come up to the front of the room and record their ratings on a poster sheet of paper. This allows for some degree of independence in rating. In addition, it minimizes a long stream of second-guessing and checking to see what others are rating the same activities.

At the same time, there is nothing confidential about the process. Program staff members and participants place their initials at the top of the matrix and then record their ratings for each activity. Contrary to most research designs, this system is designed in general to ensure that everyone knows and is influenced by each other's ratings (*after* recording them on the poster sheet). This is part of the socialization process that takes place in an empowerment evaluation, opening up the discussion and stepping toward more open disclosure—speaking one's truth.

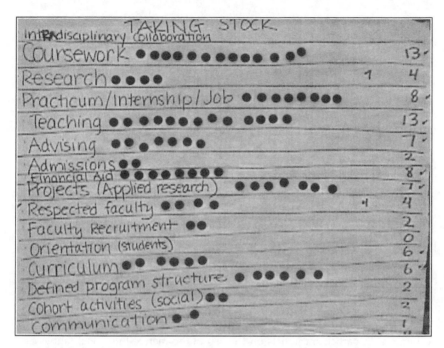

Figure 3.3. This picture captures a typical taking stock prioritization exercise. Dots are used to vote for the most significant activities in the program. The total number of dots for each activity has been added on the right-hand side of the poster. The activities with the most dots are selected for the second stage of the taking stock exercise—rating the activities.

The taking stock phase of an empowerment evaluation is conducted in an open setting for three reasons: (a) it creates a democratic flow of information and exchange of information; (b) it makes it more difficult for managers to retaliate because it is in an open forum; and (c) it increases the probability that the disclosures will be diplomatic, because program staff members and participants must remain in that environment. Open discussions in a vacuum, without regard for workplace norms, are not productive. They are often unrealistic and can be counter-productive.

Staff members and participants are more likely to give their program a higher rating if they are only asked to give an overall or gestalt rating about the program. Consequently, it is important that program staff members and participants be asked to begin by assessing individual program activities. They are more likely to give some activities low ratings if they are given an equal opportunity to speak positively about, or rate, other activi-

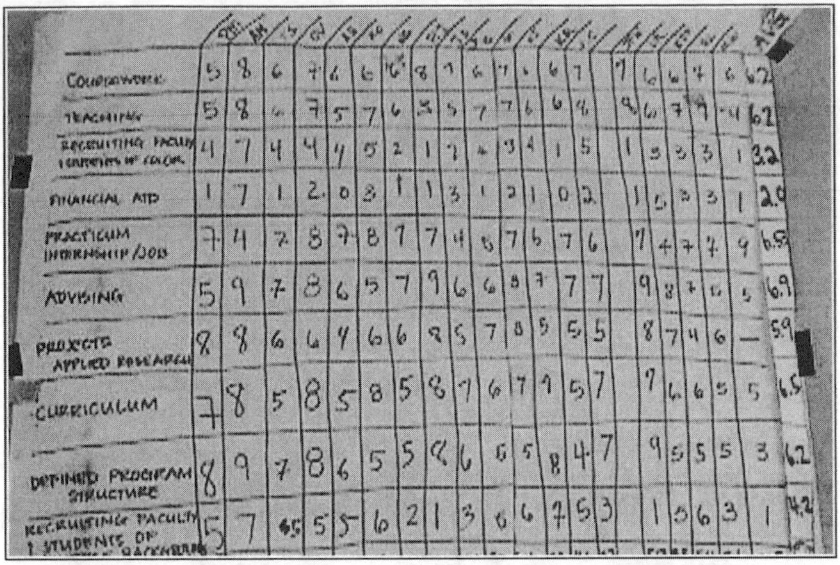

Figure 3.4. A picture of the matrix used to facilitate the second step in the taking stock stage of the empowerment evauation process. Activities are listed on the left column, with participant initials on the top of the matrix. Individual ratings are listed for each activity in the column directly below the participant's initials. The averages are recorded on the bottom and on the right-hand side of the spreadsheet. This worksheet provides a useful mechanism for entering into a dialogue about the status of the program.

ties highly. The ratings can be totaled and averaged by person and by activity. This provides some insight into routinely optimistic and pessimistic participants. It allows participants to see where they stand in relation to their peers, which helps them calibrate their own assessments in the future. The more important rating, of course, is across the matrix or spreadsheet by activity. Each activity receives a total and average. Combining the individual activity averages generates a total program rating, often lower than an external assessment rating. This represents the first baseline data concerning that specific program activity. This can be used to compare change over time.[1]

All of this work sets the tone for one of the most important parts of the empowerment evaluation process: dialogue. The empowerment evaluator facilitates a discussion about the ratings. A survey would have accomplished the same task up to this point. However, the facilitator probes and asks why one person rated communication a 6, whereas two others rated it a 3 on the matrix. Participants are asked to explain their rating and provide evidence or documentation to support the rating. This plants the seeds for the next stage of empowerment evaluation, planning for the future, where they will need to specify the evidence they plan to use to document that their activities are helping them accomplish their goals. The empowerment evaluator serves as a critical friend during this stage, facilitating discussion, making sure everyone is heard, and at the same time being critical and asking, "What do you mean by that?" or asking for additional clarification and substantiation about a particular rating or viewpoint.

Participants are asked for both the positive and negative basis for their ratings. For example, if they give communication a 3, they are asked why a 3. The typical response is because there is poor communication and they proceed to list reasons for this problem. The empowerment evaluator listens and helps record the information and then asks the question again, focusing on why it was a 3 instead of a 1. In other words, there must be something positive to report as well. An important part of empowerment evaluation involves building on strengths; even in weak areas, there is typically something positive that can be used to strengthen that activity or other activities. If the effort becomes exclusively problem focused, all participants see are difficulties instead of the strengths and opportunities to build and improve on practice.

Some participants give their programs or specific activities unrealistically high ratings. The absence of appropriate documentation, peer ratings, and a reminder about the realities of their environment—such as a high drop-out rate, students bringing guns to school, and racial violence in a high school—help participants recalibrate their ratings. Participants are reminded that they can change their ratings throughout the dialogue and exchange stage of the workshop, based on what they hear and learn from their peers. The ratings are not carved in stone. However, in some cases, ratings stay higher than peers consider appropriate. The significance of this process, however, is not the actual rating so much as it is the creation of a baseline, as noted earlier, from which future progress can be measured. In addition, it sensitizes program participants to the necessity of collecting data to support assessments or appraisals.

After examining four or five examples, beginning with divergent ones and ending with similar ratings (to determine if there are totally different reasons for the same or similar ratings), this phase of the workshop is generally complete. The group or a designated subcommittee continues to discuss the ratings, and the group is asked to return to the next workshop on planning for the future with the final ratings and a brief description or explanation of what the ratings meant. (This is normally shared with the group for review, at a time in which ratings can still be changed, and then a consensus is sought concerning the document.) This process is superior to surveys, because it generally has a higher response rate—close to 100% depending on how many staff members and participants are present—and it allows participants to discuss what they meant by their ratings, to recalibrate and revise their ratings based on what they learn, thus minimizing both the "talking past each other" about certain issues and other miscommunications, such as defining terms differently and using radically different rating systems. Participants learn what a 3 and an 8 mean to individuals in the group in the process of discussing and arguing about these ratings. This is a form of norming, helping create shared meanings and interpretations within a group.

Planning for the Future

After rating their program's performance and providing documentation to support that rating, program participants are asked, "Where do you want to go from here?" They are asked how they would like to improve on what they do well and not so well. The empowerment evaluator asks the group to use the taking stock list of activities as the basis for their plans for the future—so that their mission guides their taking stock, and the results of their taking stock shapes their planning for the future. This creates a thread of coherence and an audit trail for each step of their evaluation and action plans.

Program staff members and participants are asked to list their goals based on the results of their taking stock exercise. They set specific goals associated with each activity. Then the empowerment evaluator asks members of the group for strategies to accomplish each goal. They are also asked to generate forms of evidence to monitor progress toward specified goals. Program staff members and participants supply all of this information.

The empowerment evaluator is not superior or inferior in the process: Staff members, participants, and evaluators are equals. The empowerment evaluator adds ideas as deemed appropriate without dominating the discussion. The primary role of the evaluator is to serve as a coach, facilitator, and critical evaluative friend. The empowerment evaluator must be able to

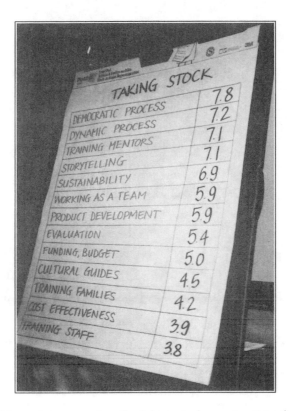

Figure 3.5. This poster summarizes the taking stock exercise. It is often used to guide the initial exercise in planning for the future. It summarizes the taking stock effort, and ranks the ratings for each activity from high to low.

serve as a facilitator, helping program members and participants process and be heard. The evaluator must also be analytical and critical, asking or prompting participants to clarify, document, and evaluate what they are doing, to ensure that specific goals are achieved. If the evaluator is only critical and analytical, the group will walk away from the endeavor. The empowerment evaluator must maintain a balance of these talents or team up with other coaches from within the group or outside the group who can help them maintain this balance.

The selected goals should be established in conjunction with supervisors and clients to ensure relevance from both perspectives. In addition,

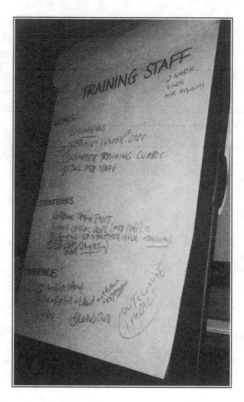

Figure 3.6. This is a planning-for-the-future poster focusing on training staff. The three categories used to organize this stage of the process are *goals, strategies,* and *evidence.* The facilitator writes the participants' ideas down in the appropriate category on these poster sheets.

goals should be realistic, taking into consideration such factors as initial conditions, motivation, resources, and program dynamics. They should also take into consideration external standards, such as accreditation agency standards, a superintendent's 5-year plan, board of trustee dictates, board standards, and so on.

In addition, it is important that goals be related to the program's activities, talents, resources, and scope of capability. One problem with traditional external evaluation is that programs have been given grandiose or long-term goals that participants could only contribute to in some indirect manner. There is often no link between an individual's daily activities and ultimate long-term program outcomes in terms of these goals. In empowerment evaluation, program participants are encouraged to select intermediate goals that are directly linked to their daily activities. These activities can then be linked to larger, more diffuse goals, creating a clear chain of reasoning and outcomes.

Program participants are encouraged to be creative in establishing their goals. A brainstorming approach is often used to generate a new set of goals. In such a process, individuals are asked to state what they think the program should be doing. The list generated from this activity is refined, reduced, and made realistic after the brainstorming phase, through a critical review and consensual agreement process.

There are a bewildering number of goals to strive for at any given time. As a group begins to establish goals based on this initial review of their program, they realize quickly that a consensus is required to determine the most significant issues to focus on. These are chosen according to (a) significance to the operation of the program, such as teaching in an educational setting; (b) timing or urgency, such as with recruitment or budget issues; and (c) vision, including community building and learning processes.

Goal setting can be a slow process when program participants have a heavy work schedule. Sensitivity to the pacing of this effort is essential. Additional tasks of any kind and for any purpose may be perceived as simply another burden when everyone is fighting to keep their heads above water. However, individuals interested in specific goals should be asked to volunteer to be responsible for them as a team leader to ensure follow-through and internal accountability.

Developing Strategies

Program participants are also responsible for selecting and developing strategies to accomplish program goals. The same process of brainstorming, critical review, and consensual agreement is used to establish a set of strategies, which are routinely reviewed to determine their effectiveness and appropriateness. Determining appropriate strategies, in consultation with sponsors and clients, is an essential part of the empowering process. Program participants are typically the most knowledgeable about their own jobs, and this approach acknowledges and uses that expertise—and, in the process, puts them back in the driver's seat.

Documenting Progress

Program staff members and participants are asked what type of documentation or evidence is required to monitor progress toward their goals. This is a critical step. Each form of documentation is scrutinized for relevance to avoid devoting time to collecting information that will not be useful or pertinent. Program participants are asked to explain how a given form of documentation is related to specific program goals. This review process is difficult and time-consuming, but prevents wasted time and disillusionment at the end of the process. In addition, documentation must be credible and rigorous if it is to withstand the criticism that this evaluation is self-serving. (For additional discussion on this topic, see Fetterman, 1994b.)

The entire process of establishing a mission, taking stock, and planning for the future creates an implicit logic model or program theory, demonstrating how there is nothing as practical as a good theory of action, especially one grounded in participants' own experiences. (For additional discussion about program theory, see Bickman, 1987; Chen, 1990; Connell, Kubisch, Schorr, & Weiss, 1995; Cook & Shadish, 1994; McClintock, 1990; Patton, 1989; Weiss, 1998; Wholey, 1987.) The facets of empowerment evaluation represent a metatheory of the approach based on actual practice.

■ Facets of Empowerment Evaluation

Training, facilitation, advocacy, illumination, and liberation are all facets—if not developmental stages—of empowerment evaluation. The emphasis is on program development, improvement, and lifelong learning. These facets or demarcation points help empowerment evaluators know where they are along the continuum of empowerment evaluation. They should be viewed as similar to a Maslowian hierarchy, as developmental stages or building blocks. Training and facilitation are the most fundamental forms of interaction in empowerment evaluation. They build a foundation on which the remaining facets or development stages can emerge. Once program staff members and participants learn how to assess themselves, they can use the findings for advocacy. In addition, being a part of the evaluation process is a precondition for illumination and liberation. A metaevaluation of an empowerment evaluation can use these facets as benchmarks to determine the type or level of empowerment evaluation observed. They can also be used to assess the developmental stage of an empowerment evaluation appropriately.

Training

In one facet of empowerment evaluation, evaluators teach people to conduct their own evaluations and thus become more self-sufficient. This approach desensitizes and demystifies evaluation, and ideally helps organizations internalize evaluation principles and practices, making evaluation an integral part of program planning. Too often, an external evaluation is an exercise in dependency rather than an empowering experience: In these instances, the process ends when the evaluator departs, leaving participants without the knowledge or experience to continue for themselves. In contrast, an evaluation conducted by program participants is designed to be ongoing and internalized in the system, creating the opportunity for capacity building.

In empowerment evaluation, training is used to map out the terrain, highlighting categories and concerns. It is also used in making preliminary assessments of program components, while also illustrating the need to establish goals, strategies to achieve goals, and documentation to indicate or substantiate progress. Training a group to conduct a self-evaluation can be considered equivalent to developing an evaluation or research design (as that is the core of the training), a standard part of any evaluation. This training is ongoing, because new skills are needed to respond to new levels of understanding. Training also becomes part of the self-reflective process of self-assessment (on a program level) in that participants must learn to recognize when more tools are required to continue and enhance the evaluation process. This self-assessment process is pervasive in an empowerment evaluation; it is built into every part of a program, even to the point of reflecting on how its own meetings are conducted and feeding that input into future practice.

In essence, empowerment evaluation takes the concept *Give someone a fish and you feed her for a day; teach her to fish, and she will feed herself for the rest of her life* and applies it to evaluation. The primary difference is that in empowerment evaluation the evaluator and the individuals benefiting from the evaluation are typically on an even plane, learning from each other. (For a sample of useful training tools, see Dugan, 1996; Fetterman, 1998a; Linney & Wandersman, 1991, 1996; Mayer, 1996.)

Facilitation

Empowerment evaluators serve as coaches or facilitators to help others conduct a self-evaluation. In my role as a coach, I provide general guidance and direction to the effort, attending sessions to monitor and facilitate as needed. It is critical to emphasize that staff members and participants are in charge of their effort; otherwise, program staff members and participants initially tend to look to the empowerment evaluator as expert, which makes them dependent on an outside agent. In some instances, my task is to clear away obstacles and identify and clarify miscommunication patterns. I also participate in many meetings along with internal empowerment evaluators, providing explanations, suggestions, and advice at various junctures to help ensure that the process has a fair chance. (For an example of working with an internal team, see Fetterman, 1996a, p. 11.)

An empowerment evaluation coach can also provide useful information about how to create facilitation teams (balancing analytical and social skills discussed briefly earlier), work with resistant (but interested) units, develop refresher sessions to energize tired units, and resolve various protocol issues. Simple suggestions along these lines can keep an effort from backfiring or being seriously derailed. A coach may also be asked to help create the evaluation design with minimal additional support.

Whatever the contribution, the empowerment evaluation coach must ensure that the evaluation remains in the hands of program personnel. The coach's task is to provide useful information, based on her evaluator's training and past experience, to keep the effort on course.

Advocacy

A common workplace practice discussed earlier provides a familiar illustration of self-evaluation and its link to advocacy on an individual level. Employees often collaborate with both supervisor and client to establish both goals and strategies for achieving those goals and documenting progress on realistic time lines. Employees collect data on their own performance, and present their case for their performance appraisal. Self-evaluation thus becomes a tool of advocacy. This individual self-evaluation process is easily transferable to the group or program level.

Sponsors and program administrators invest in a program, and would like to see a return on their investment. They are not interested in requests for a blank check or a free ride from program staff members or participants.

They are interested in seeing appropriate processes and specific outcomes. They are typically interested in funding programs that can demonstrate effectiveness. Program staff members and participants are in a better position to request funding when they have the data; specifically a record of desired results they can share with sponsors and administrators. Program staff members and participants are also in a better position to share negative findings about performance with a sponsor and request funding to improve their performance when they can demonstrate how effective they have been with funded efforts. These are forms of legitimate advocacy. As Mills wrote in 1959,

> There is no necessity for working social scientists to allow the potential meaning of their work to be shaped by the "accidents of its setting," or its use to be determined by the purposes of other men [or women]. It is quite within their powers to discuss its meaning and decide upon its use as matters of their own policy. (p. 177)

The same sentiment applies to program staff members and participants as they engage in the process of self-evaluation and chart their own future. (For examples of research and evaluation-based advocacy, see Fetterman, 1993b, 1996a; Hess, 1993; Hopper, 1993; Parker & Langley, 1993; Weeks & Schensul, 1993.)

Illumination

Illumination is an eye-opening, revealing, and enlightening experience. Typically, a new insight or understanding about roles, structures, and program dynamics is developed in the process of determining worth and striving for program improvement (see Partlett & Hamilton, 1976). Empowerment evaluation is illuminating on a number of levels. For example, an administrator in one empowerment evaluation, with little or no research background, developed a testable, researchable hypothesis in the middle of a discussion about indicators and self-evaluation. It was not only illuminating to the group (and to her), but also revealed what they could do as a group when given the opportunity to think about problems and come up with workable options, hypotheses, and tests. This experience of illumination holds the same intellectual intoxication each of us experienced the first time we came up with a researchable question. This experience also applies to evaluators trained in another tradition who suddenly see the power of this approach. As one colleague exclaimed in the middle of a presentation, "I get it: It is not formative, it is transformative! " The process creates a dynamic community of learners (for all of us), as people engage in the art and science of evaluating themselves. (For additional examples, see Fetterman, 1996a, pp. 15–16; see also Chapter 4 for case examples.)

Liberation

Illumination often sets the stage for liberation. It can unleash powerful, emancipatory forces for self-determination. Liberation is the act of being freed or freeing oneself from preexisting roles and constraints. It often involves new conceptualizations of oneself and others. Empowerment evaluation can also be liberating. Many of the examples in this discussion demonstrate how helping individuals take charge of their lives—and find useful ways to evaluate themselves—liberates them from traditional expectations and roles. They also demonstrate how empowerment evaluation enables participants to find new opportunities, see existing resources in a new light, and redefine their identities and future roles.

For example, school nurses in the Oakland Public School system used this approach to help them understand their own evolving role in the school district. They are highly educated professionals; however, they were underutilized, placing band-aids on children's arms. The contrast of such a highly educated work force with menial tasks conflicted with their own sense of self-worth and the administration's financial capacity to support them. The nurses used empowerment evaluation to help define their role in the future. Instead of focusing exclusively on individual children, they became more involved in assessing the life circumstances of the entire student population. This liberated them from their highly confining roles. It also enabled them to generate more effective efforts, which were appreciated and valued by the administration. For example, instead of providing a generic health program throughout the district (with little impact), they developed highly specific health packages targeting issues such as asthma and AIDS. This targeted approach was more effective than a generic health care approach. Administrators appreciated the change because it demonstrated specific measurable outcomes (which also made them look good).

Liberation takes on another level of significance when working in townships in South Africa. Community members are using empowerment

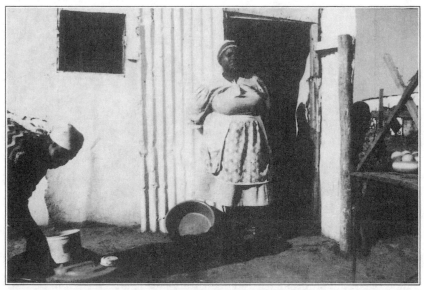

Figure 3.7. A South African woman standing in front of her home in a community where significant self-help development efforts have been initiated.

Figure 3.8. The housing and sanitary conditions captured in this photograph provide a measure of the scope of the problem facing disenfranchised South African communities after Apartheid.

Figure 3.9. Some of my South African colleagues working as a team to respond to a variety of community health needs ranging from smoking to hypertension.

evaluation with a broad range of community participation health care programs.

They use self-evaluation to monitor and build on successes and failures. This commendable work takes place in a context of poverty and violence (Fetterman, 1993a).

Program staff members and participants engage in personally liberating experiences every day, given the backdrop of Apartheid. Many of their daily activities, particularly those associated with self-determination and taking your life into your own hands, were illegal before Apartheid was abolished. One impoverished black community near Cape Town is implementing and evaluating smoking cessation, hypertension, and teenage pregnancy prevention programs. This progressive, self-reflective community mirrors the real spirit of hope for democracy and the reconstruction of South Africa.

It should also be noted that liberation applies to the empowerment evaluator in evaluations. I recall one township meeting where I had a suggestion about how to design the community gardens for self-sufficiency, and was told, "Not right now, David." A traditional evaluator might have viewed this as an inefficient use of resources—a failure to use the evaluator from another continent. Personally, the traditional evaluator might have

Figure 3.10. The director of the program and I consulting about plans for the community, focusing on self-sufficiency.

been insulted. However, as an empowerment evaluator, I viewed this experience with great pleasure. They were "getting it." They did not need me in the same way anymore; they were taking charge of their own lives. This can be a liberating experience for an evaluator, as we learn a new, less dominant but more powerful role: nurturing and fostering self-determination.

■ Conclusion

The steps of empowerment evaluation are simple and effective. They help systematize the self-evaluation process, while leaving it in the hands of program staff members and participants. The facets and stages of empowerment evaluation help evaluators and program participants place markers at critical stages or levels of development. They can be used as meta-evaluation criteria when determining how effective this emancipatory approach to evaluation is or what level it has reached. Case examples are presented in the next chapter to further illuminate the steps and facets of empowerment evaluation.

■ Notes

1. Program staff members and participants should return to these activity ratings on a routine basis. In some cases, a monthly comparison is needed. However, most programs return to these ratings at a 3-, 6-, or 12-month interval.

FOUR CASE EXAMPLES

Highlighting the Steps of Empowerment Evaluation With Four Case Examples

Few things are harder to put up with than the annoyance of a good example.

—Mark Twain

The steps of empowerment evaluation are more meaningful when illustrated with case examples. Therefore, four case examples in diverse settings have been selected to demonstrate how these steps function in practice. The first is a children's hospital, the second a reading improvement program, the third an Upward Bound program, and the fourth a summer school program.

■ Hospital

A project team in one of the most prestigious children's hospitals in the country has been using empowerment evaluation to help make the hospital more family centered. They spent over a year working on initial planning and mission-related activities before inviting the empowerment evaluation team to assist them. However, in a 3-hour empowerment evaluation session they crystallized their mission and took stock of their program activities in this area. The empowerment evaluation team consisted of Ellie Fischbacher, Katherine Rynearson, and myself. I provided the initial workshop facilitation sessions, and Ellie Fischbacher and Katherine Rynearson provided ongoing support by attending meetings, recording activities, conducting follow-up activities, and suggesting options and strategies to help the group achieve their objectives.

The first phase followed the traditional format in which program members and participants, including parents, provided their views about the mission. This allowed new members of the group to have a voice, senior members to observe concrete changes or shifts in the focus of the group as it had matured, and forced the group to put some closure on this phase of their activities. The draft mission statement is as follows:

> Our mission is to inspire cultural change throughout the hospital by creating dynamic partnerships between families and professionals. We seek to incorporate multiple perspectives of health and healing into a new vision for family-centered care. We strive to reduce the trauma of hospitalization, support family relationships, and include parents' perspectives in shaping hospital policy by encouraging collaboration and providing access to health care that is flexible and responsive to families' needs. We are committed to supporting and training staff so that they develop a common understanding of family-centered care principles for use in practice.
>
> Our vision is that family-centered care at [the hospital] will continue to evolve over time through the combined efforts of parents, health care providers, and administrators who will together create an environment that supports ongoing transdisciplinary process, provides opportunities for transformative learning, and stimulates the generation of innovative practices at all levels of health care delivery.

The next step involved taking stock, which consisted of the following substeps: (a) brainstorming a list of key activities associated with the proj-

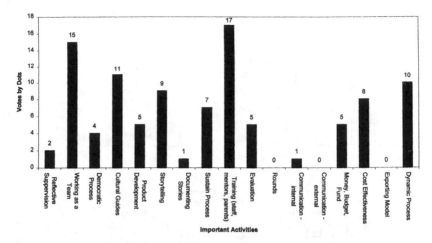

Figure 4.1. Hospital Empowerment Evaluation: Taking Stock (Phase I)—Key Activities.

ect; (b) prioritizing the list of key activities; (c) rating each activity (on a 1 to 10 point scale); and (d) discussing what the ratings meant.

The first step went smoothly, as a long list of critical activities was generated. Then the list was prioritized by giving members of the group five dot stickers to place on any activity or set of activities they thought were most important to program operations. This can be visually represented on a poster sheet of paper with dots clustered around each activity or later transformed into a bar chart highlighting the prioritization in a commonly understood fashion (see Figure 4.1).

After the activities were prioritized, the top 10 were listed and project members rated each activity. Then I, as one of the empowerment evaluators, facilitated a discussion or dialogue about the ratings (see Figures 4.2 and 4.3).

These documents provide the participants with a written record of their assessment, a guide for future actions, and a socializing tool to help new members understand the group's priorities and where they are in their efforts. The matrix or spreadsheet document highlights overall average ratings by activity and by person. In addition, it pulls out explanations or points made about each of the critical ratings discussed during the workshop.

One of the empowerment evaluators in this project created a Power-Point presentation as a vehicle to record participant comments about indi-

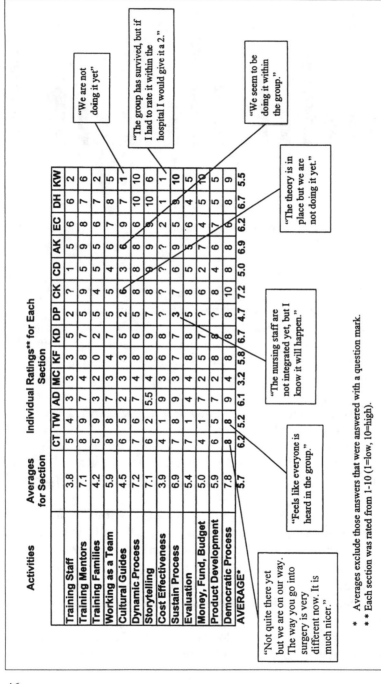

Activities	Averages for Section	Individual Ratings** for Each Section												
		CT	TW	AD	MC	KF	KD	DP	CK	CD	AK	EC	DH	KW
Training Staff	3.8	5	4	3	3	3	5	2	?	1	5	6	6	2
Training Mentors	7.1	8	9	7	4	8	7	5	9	5	9	8	7	6
Training Families	4.2	5	9	3	2	0	2	5	4	5	5	6	7	2
Working as a Team	5.9	8	8	7	3	4	7	5	5	4	6	7	8	5
Cultural Guides	4.5	6	5	2	3	3	5	2	5	3	6	9	7	1
Dynamic Process	7.2	7	6	7	4	8	6	5	8	8	8	6	10	10
Storytelling	7.1	6	2	5.5	4	8	9	7	8	9	9	9	10	6
Cost Effectiveness	3.9	4	1	9	3	6	8	?	8	?	?	2	1	1
Sustain Process	6.9	7	8	9	3	7	7	3	7	6	9	5	9	10
Evaluation	5.4	7	1	4	4	8	8	5	8	5	6	6	4	5
Money, Fund, Budget	5.0	4	1	7	2	5	7	?	6	2	7	4	5	10
Product Development	5.9	6	5	7	2	8	8	?	8	4	6	7	5	5
Democratic Process	7.8	8	9	9	4	8	8	8	10	8	8	8	8	9
AVERAGE*	5.7	6.2	5.2	6.1	3.2	5.8	6.7	4.7	7.2	5.0	6.9	6.2	6.7	5.5

"We are not doing it yet"

"The group has survived, but if I had to rate it within the hospital I would give it a 2."

"We seem to be doing it within the group."

"The theory is in place but we are not doing it yet."

"The nursing staff are not integrated yet, but I know it will happen."

"Feels like everyone is heard in the group."

"Not quite there yet but we are on our way. The way you go into surgery is very different now. It is much nicer."

* Averages exclude those answers that were answered with a question mark.
** Each section was rated from 1-10 (1=low, 10=high).

Figure 4.2. Hospital Empowerment Evaluation: Taking Stock (Phase II)—Rating the Activities.

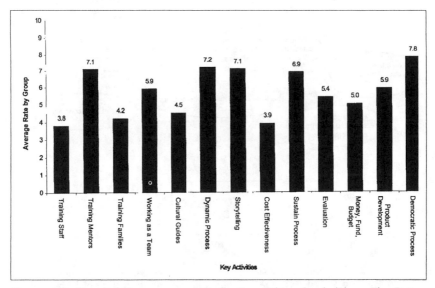

Figure 4.3. Hospital Empowerment Evaluation: Taking Stock (Phase II)—Rating the Activities Bar Chart.

vidual ratings and group assessments about critical activities. This format also stimulated and guided additional dialogue about participants' views and the status of the project. The activities and processes most meriting evaluation according to the program staff included training staff, training families/mentors, working as a team, cultivating cultural guides, maintaining a dynamic process, storytelling, becoming cost effective and sustainable, evaluating the program, securing funding, product development, and instituting and maintaining a democratic process. See Figures 4.4–4.15 for the PowerPoint illustrations.

The circles in each of these figures provided an insight into the divergent views represented by group members. It helped them to norm or use common terms and standards for their assessments. Storytelling or telling your story about what worked and what did not work in the process of trying to make the hospital a more family-centered institution became a critical activity associated with learning, socializing new parents, and providing sustainability (keeping members in the group). The ratings associated with cost effectiveness, sustainability, and funding demonstrated the sensitivity of hospital program staff members and patients to the reality of operating in a hospital—the fiscal context.

(text continues on page 54)

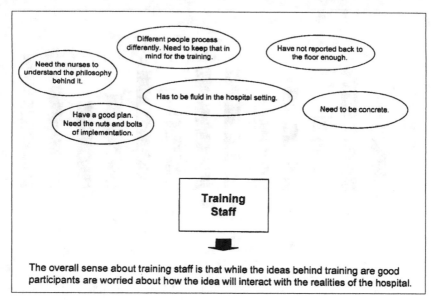

Figure 4.4. Hospital Empowerment Evaluation: PowerPoint Presentation—Training Staff.

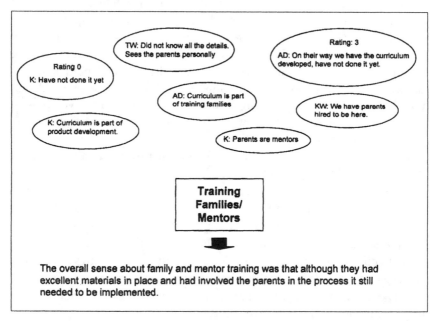

Figure 4.5. Hospital Empowerment Evaluation: PowerPoint Presentation—Training Families/Mentors.

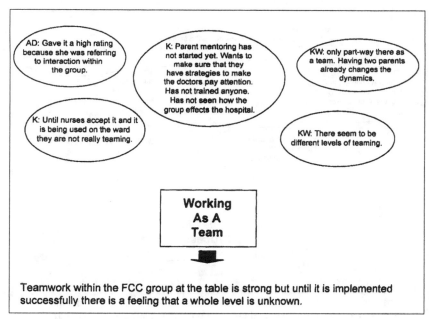

Figure 4.6. Hospital Empowerment Evaluation: PowerPoint Presentation—Working as a Team.

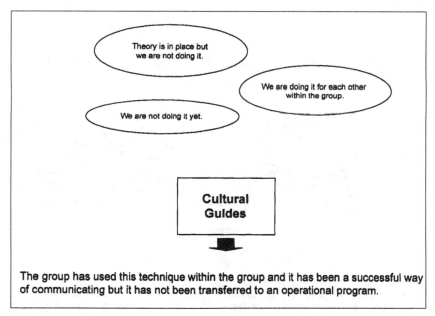

Figure 4.7. Hospital Empowerment Evaluation: PowerPoint Presentation—Cultural Guides.

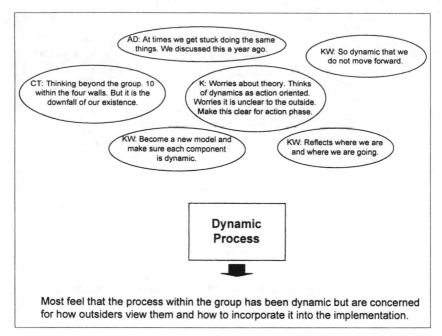

Figure 4.8. Hospital Empowerment Evaluation: PowerPoint Presentation—Dynamic Process.

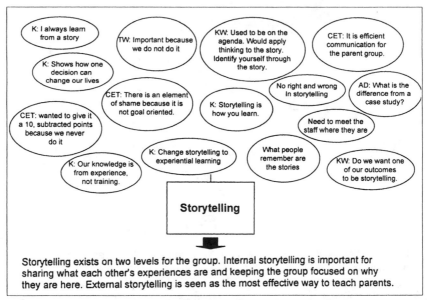

Figure 4.9. Hospital Empowerment Evaluation: PowerPoint Presentation—Storytelling.

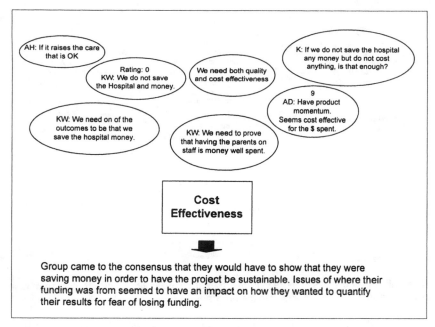

Figure 4.10. Hospital Empowerment Evaluation: PowerPoint Presentation—Cost Effectiveness.

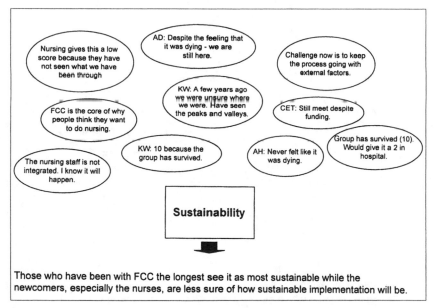

Figure 4.11. Hospital Empowerment Evaluation: PowerPoint Presentation—Sustainability.

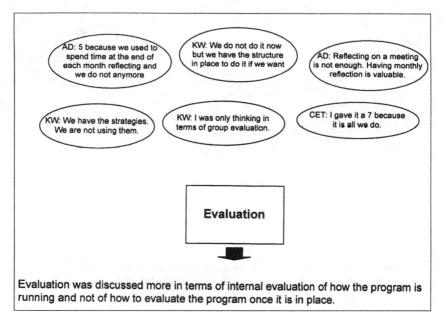

Figure 4.12. Hospital Empowerment Evaluation: PowerPoint Presentation—Evaluation.

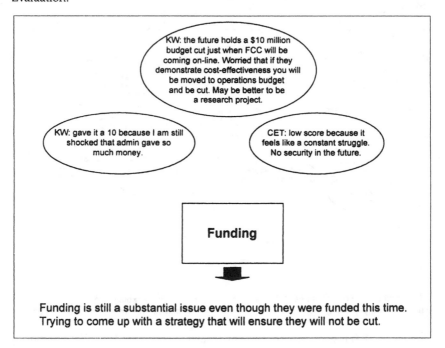

Figure 4.13. Hospital Empowerment Evaluation: PowerPoint Presentation—Funding.

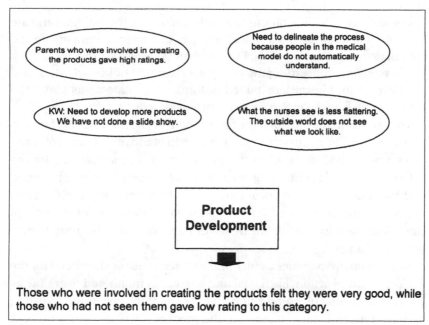

Figure 4.14. Hospital Empowerment Evaluation: PowerPoint Presentation— Product Development.

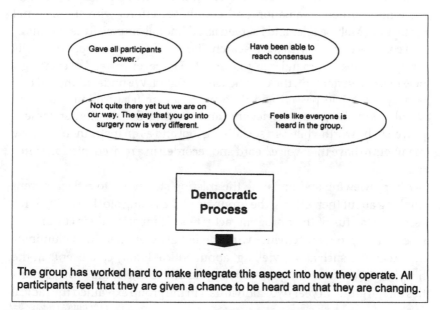

Figure 4.15. Hospital Empowerment Evaluation: PowerPoint Presentation— Democratic Process.

These charts and illustrations are useful records of the dialogue and are helpful tools in preparing a more complete document summarizing the overall rationale for the ratings. The bar chart (Figure 4.3) provided a quick visual reference concerning the group's assessment of key activities, and the PowerPoint illustrations pulled out individual statements about the ratings as well as the group's summary assessment.

These documents provided the foundation for the third stage: planning for the future. The discussion about key activities and the rationale for various ratings provided the seeds for the next stage. In the planning for the future stage, participants were asked to identify specific goals, strategies, and forms of evidence to document change over time—for each activity. Many of these ideas came from the taking stock dialogue. An example of the initial planning document that was generated by this group is presented in Tables 4.1–4.12.

This document provides a quick and easy reference or shorthand for the project's plan of action. Each goal and strategy is monitored over time as part of the normal planning and management of the group, internalizing and institutionalizing evaluation in the process.

The team configuration changed in the second year of the empowerment evaluation. The team hired a full-time research director to facilitate the empowerment evaluation and coordinate efforts with the external evaluation. Melissa Eiler and I served as additional empowerment evaluation coaches to work with the research director. The workshops and facilitation activities were similar to past efforts. However, instead of creating a new mission statement, the old one was revisited. We updated the old one because time had passed and there were a significant number of new members in the group. Reviewing and revising the mission statement proved to be worthwhile as a socializing tool and as an instrument for new members to have their voice heard and recorded in a revised mission statement.

After reviewing and updating the mission statement to reflect current thinking about their efforts, the group used the taking stock activity to reassess the status of their program activities. Comparing their current assessment of program activities with the initial assessment was illuminating. Activities such as storytelling[1] about critical family care events in the hospital shifted from a high priority in year one to one of the lowest priorities for the group in year two. Individuals in the group explained the radical

(text continues on page 59)

Table 4.1	Plans for the Future: Training Staff	
Goals	*Strategies*	*Evidence*
Consensus as to what Family Centered Care is Include medical staff Complete training curriculum	Formal training pilot Identify critical people (medical staff) Ongoing training Grouped by discipline or multidisciplinary? Experiential studies	Attendance checklist for training Pre- and post-test using Likert scale Video Training materials

Table 4.2	Planning for the Future: Training Mentors	
Goals	*Strategies*	*Evidence*
Train junior mentors Plan transitions (sustainability) Train parents for policy positions Make a training video	Pilot curriculum Experiential studies Assign mentor at time of diagnosis Monthly meetings Quarterly training Training parent policy mentoring (shadowing)	Pre- and post-test Families involved in hospital policymaking Document number of committees with parent participants Materials to document training, curriculum, program awareness Video debriefing Parents use time with doctors efficiently

Table 4.3	Planning for the Future: Cost Effectiveness	
Goals	*Strategies*	*Evidence*
Decrease hospital stay More efficient use of time spent with doctors Decrease emergency admits Stay within budget Enhance parent critical thinking Reduce stress for all team members Increase family satisfaction	Review Family Plan Training staff, families Monitoring implementation (Evaluation) Chart reviews Track calls to health providers, parent mentors	Family Plan checked Satisfied families Parent mentors record phone calls Children spend less time in hospital Fewer emergency admissions Decreased number of calls to health providers

(text continues on page 59)

Table 4.4	Planning for the Future: Product Development	
Goals	Strategies	Evidence
Mentor training products, notebook	Nurses to review staff and training notebook and inpatient and discharge materials	Notebook
		Section in notebook on planning process
Create family-centered care pathway		Curriculum
Research design	Enlist parents to help write parent mentor materials	Inpatient plan
Parent mentor handbook/ training		Pamphlet
	Karen and Amy create pamphlet	Inpatient plan
Staff training curriculum		Pamphlet
Family training curriculum	Identify and follow web-page protocol with controlled access	Video
Document planning process		Training materials
Create web page		Research design
Create pamphlet	Contract with videographer	Web page
Create videos	Laura, Wayne, Karen, Ann document research process	Hospital plan
Create care plan		Discharge interview
Create discharge interview	Flesh out steps for planning process	Family-centered care plan
Create family-centered care plan summary		
	Meet with Ann to add outpatient element	
Create outpatient plan to include in care plan	Physicians, house staff review and create staff training materials for residents and clinicians	

Table 4.5	Planning for the Future: Cultural Collaborations Modeling for Parents, Nurses, and Staff on How to Be Family Centered	
Goals	Strategies	Evidence
Multilevel mentoring (parents, staff, health care providers) creating cultural bridges	Have a cultural guide in each discipline	Satisfaction with the partnership, including problem solving and the decision-making process
	Identify areas of expansion and expand	
Create more connections between cultures (family, family-centered care, health care providers)	Subcommittees	Cultural guides participate in family-centered care rounds, surgical rounds
	Structure it in a way that works for different groups	
	Large group orientation for new members from mixed disciplines	Attendance and minutes from subcommittees
Create more cultural guides in each subculture		Videos of interactions
	Monthly meetings for subcultures	Pre- and postmeasures
	Family-centered care	Discharge interview of staff and families
	Large group orientation for new members from mixed disciplines	Joint decision-making
	Monthly meetings for subcultures	
	Family-centered care rounds to model behavior	
	Cross-disciplinary shadowing	

Table 4.6   Planning for the Future: Experiential Studies

Goals	Strategies	Evidence
Venue for family-centered care issues (in nursing) using reflective supervision	Bring professional stories to families and family stories to professionals	System changes based on individual experiences
Develop a reflective supervisor	Set up time for family-centered care issues in nursing	Meeting minutes
Bimonthly case presentations at house, staff, teaching rounds	Karen facilitates training of reflective supervisor in nursing	Attendance at training
Case studies presented to residents	Create training for staff members	Gather testimonials and themes from qualitative interviews regarding reflective supervision
Families talk to residents	Shadowing and reporting to Friday morning meeting	
Families aware of health care provider perspective	Karen attends Friday surgery rounds	
	Investigate house staff teaching rounds and designate someone to attend	

Table 4.7   Planning for the Future: Partnerships Working as a Team

Goals	Strategies	Evidence
Joint decision making	Hire another parent professional	Attendance lists from meetings and rounds
Parent professional representation in decision making	Attend meetings	Videotape to document interaction and quality
Adapt family-centered care theory and principles to new groups (nurses, transplant staff, families)	Designate family-centered care time during rounds	Focus groups
	Demonstrate parent competency	
	Articulate family-centered care absence at meetings	

Table 4.8   Planning for the Future: Democratic Process

Goals	Strategies	Evidence
People feel their opinion is equally valued	Open discussion about issues before decision making	Meeting minutes
Equal participation and voice	Allow time for valuing culture and opinions of others	Dilemma notes
Spread democratic process in interdisciplinary rounds and nurses' meetings	Use Eva Thorpe's version of dilemma resolution when conflict occurs	Outside evaluation of Friday meetings, meetings, interdisciplinary rounds
Maintain democratic process at Friday meetings		

Table 4.9   Planning for the Future: Dynamic Process Translating Theory Into Action: Interpersonal Transformation at the Individual

Goals	Strategies	Evidence
Develop a framework to determine whether one's own behavior is family centered	Present case studies Reflective supervision Reflection time during nurses' meetings Open-ended survey	Interviews Pre- and post-testing Self-reporting by participants

Table 4.10   Planning for the Future: Evaluation (Extended Family Formative Evaluation Process), A Meta-analysis

Goals	Strategies	Evidence
Have monthly meetings Remain flexible and responsive to the nees of the project Support integration of the project into the hospital setting	Make new key questions (e.g., Which components are working/not working? What is our relationship with administration? What would we change?) Ask questions at hot topic/ monthly summation meetings Catherine's dilemma note taking Case studies	Dilemma notes Meeting minutes Meeting attendance

Table 4.11   Planning for the Future: Money, Funding, Budget

Goals	Strategies	Evidence
Expand funding sources Maintain some Children's Hospital Initiative funding Stay within budget Collaborate with UCSF Special Program Collaborate with Dartmouth	Investigate how to get money outside of Children's Hospital Initiative (protocol) Track expenses (weekly) Karen participates on Children's Hospital Initiative committee Meet with UCSF Visit Dartmouth	Funding from Children's Hospital Initiative Funding from outside sources Collaborative grant submitted to LEND Collaborative grant submitted with Dartmouth Balanced budget

Table 4.12	Planning for the Future: Sustainability	
Goals	*Strategies*	*Evidence*
Exist next year	Data collection	Refunding
Participation at unit level	Training for unit staff	Attendance at meetings
(inpatient)	Family-centered care staff	Longitudinal ratings of
Participation at community	availability for support	importance of family-
level (outreach sites)	Recruit new families to	centered care
National awareness of	enter program	Growth of family-centered
program	Establish communication	care subcommittees
Develop training center	with outreach MDs and	Doctors refer patients to
Participants invested at	nurses	family-centered care
implementation team	Write articles	Site managers are maintained
level	Present at conferences	Invitations to National IFCC
	Connect with ACCH; parent	conference, present at
	representative at national	ACCH, attend Gore confer-
	conference	ence
	Connect with Gores	We host a conference
	Connect with IFCC	Train outsiders
	Finish notebook and materi-	Monthly hot topic meeting
	als for presentation	attendance
	Monthly hot topics meetings	

shift in priorities in the following manner: "Storytelling has been incorporated into our conversations; it is now implicit, whereas before it was explicit." As a facilitator, I noted that this marked or symbolized a transition
in the group. During the initial phases of the collaborative effort, it had
been necessary to devote focused time to developing this part of the process; however, the group reached its goal of integrating storytelling into
their discourse by the second year. It also represented a difference between
the new and old members of the group. The original group defined their
identity in terms of these personal stories in which members "poured out
their hearts" about key events in the hospital. The new group did not feel
the need for the same level of culture-building techniques, and preferred a
more efficient manner of communicating about the team's work in the
hospital. Identifying the characteristics of this transition, including the
tensions associated with it, was helpful in maintaining group cohesion.

A review of the original plans for the future helped the group focus on
accomplishments and goals requiring additional attention. In addition, it

set the foundation and tone for the group's efforts in creating an updated future plan, reflecting both the past plans and current priorities, initiatives, and organizational changes (e.g., the hospital merger). A formal comparison with the original mission statement, taking stock document, and planning for the future outlines helped the collaborative effort stay on track, as well as recharge and refocus their efforts.

■ Reading Program

A school-based reading improvement program provides the context for the next case example. Jane Cooper and I served as empowerment evaluators in this effort. This group followed the same pattern of generating a mission statement or set of values to guide their work. In this case, a fair amount of time was devoted to the mission statement. I facilitated a public critique of it, which was extremely useful because it involved students, program administrators, and funders. There was a significant conflict in worldviews about who the program was designed to serve that emerged from this process. The university-based students, operating the reading program, thought it was designed as a service program to assist students in the community who were having difficulty reading, whereas the program administrators and funders focused on the service opportunity it provided for university students implementing the program. The administrators explained how the primary rationale had to be what the program was doing for students running the program, given it was operating under the institution's umbrella and had to conform to the mission or purpose of the educational institution. Otherwise it would not be able to justify support to this service activity as compared with some other worthy service activity. The process of sharing different worldviews was an eye-opening experience for most of the university students. It provided a diametrically opposite position or view of reality from their understanding of their mission. Their new mission statement reflects both their new understanding and the dual and potentially conflicting tensions and allegiances underlying the program:

> The Caring Community Reads Program[2] embraces two primary goals—one focuses on University-based student tutors and one on the needs of the elementary school students with whom they work.

The first goal of Caring Community Reads Program is to increase the students' reading abilities—to assist an elementary school child in reaching or surpassing grade level reading competencies. Elementary school students meet with a tutor several times a week for one-on-one instruction that supplements what has already been taught in the classroom. Tutors are trained to *teach* a structured curriculum *with emphasis on* phonemic awareness, reading comprehension, and vocabulary development. *The tutoring sessions result in the added benefit of developing self-confidence in the children.*

The second goal is in keeping with one of the objectives of the University Public Service Center mission: to enhance University student classroom studies by participation in a broad range of community experiences supported by the University Public Service Center and affiliated organizations. The Caring Community Reads tutor *has* an opportunity to experience and learn about the greater social context in which they study and live. Tutors *are introduced to* the life of an educator, through first-hand observations and regular interactions with *elementary* school staff and faculty. The University student learns by serving as a mentor, teacher, confidant, and role model to the child he/she tutors. Tutors attain and hone leadership, interpersonal, teaching, and organizational skills through this service experience.

The partnership that has developed between the University and the local community School District in the form of Caring Community Reads supports a learning environment for University students and local school children. Our hope is that this program becomes a model for use within other schools in the local community School District, in other elementary districts, and on other university campuses throughout the nation.

The group took this step of creating a mission statement very seriously, and devoted time in small groups as well as in the workshops to wordsmithing this document to reflect the diverse set of values represented by the entire group.

The Caring Community Reads Program also followed the same format in generating a list of critical program activities, prioritizing them, rating each activity, and then discussing their ratings and the activities in greater depth. Their taking stock document or matrix with "pull-out boxes" to highlight their rationale for their ratings is provided in Figure 4.16, followed by a bar chart in Figure 4.17 to highlight the ratings in another for-

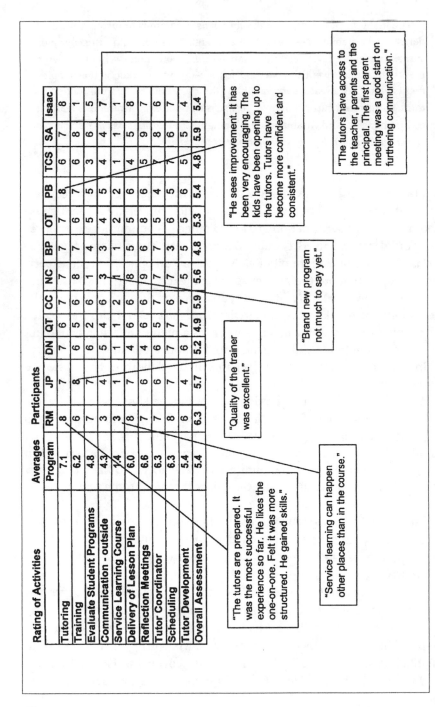

Rating of Activities	Averages	Participants											
	Program	RM	JP	DN	QT	CC	NC	BP	OT	PB	TCS	SA	Isaac
Tutoring	7.1	8	7	7	6	7	7	7	7	8	6	7	8
Training	6.2	6	8	6	5	6	8	7	6	7	6	8	1
Evaluate Student Programs	4.8	7	7	6	2	6	1	4	5	5	3	6	5
Communication - outside	4.3	3	4	5	4	6	3	3	4	5	4	4	7
Service Learning Course	1.4	3	1	1	1	2	1	1	2	2	1	1	1
Delivery of Lesson Plan	6.0	8	6	4	6	6	8	5	5	6	4	5	8
Reflection Meetings	6.6	7	6	4	6	6	9	6	8	6	5	9	7
Tutor Coordinator	6.3	7	7	6	5	7	7	7	5	4	7	8	6
Scheduling	6.3	8	7	7	7	6	7	3	6	5	5	6	7
Tutor Development	5.4	6	4	6	7	7	5	5	5	6	5	5	4
Overall Assessment	5.4	6.3	5.7	5.2	4.9	5.9	5.6	4.8	5.3	5.4	4.8	5.9	5.4

"The tutors are prepared. It was the most successful experience so far. He likes the one-on-one. Felt it was more structured. He gained skills."

"Service learning can happen other places than in the course."

"Quality of the trainer was excellent."

"Brand new program not much to say yet."

"He sees improvement. It has been very encouraging. The kids have been opening up to the tutors. Tutors have become more confident and consistent."

"The tutors have access to the teacher, parents and the principal. The first parent meeting was a good start on furthering communication."

Figure 4.16. Caring Community Reads Program Evaluation: Taking Stock—Matrix.

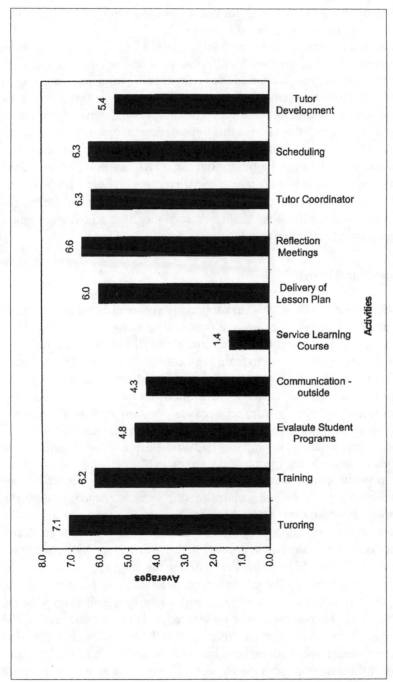

Figure 4.17. Caring Community Reads Program Evaluation: Taking Stock—Bar Chart.

mat, recognizing that no single format works for everyone to facilitate understanding and organizational learning.

This information was used as baseline data to compare changes over time. It should be noted that this effort was not without difficulty. The director of the program was ambivalent about self-evaluation, resulting in various passive-aggressive behaviors and mixed messages. Very little progress was made for months, until Jane Cooper sat down with the director and highlighted the value of this information to inform decision making. Jane Cooper specifically helped the director see the link between evaluation data and future funding: advocacy. The director had an "aha" moment during this last exchange, and then came on board 100%. In this case, patience, persistence, and hard work paid off. Their plans for the future step followed the same basic format of identifying goals, strategies, and evidence to monitor and document change over time.

■ Upward Bound

The Upward Bound case was an emotionally powerful experience. Sandra Paik and I served as empowerment evaluation coaches in this evaluation. The program was designed to help inner-city, disenfranchised minority students make the transition from high school to college. The program staff members did not trust their university-based administrative supervisors and sponsors. The supervisors and sponsors were reaching the point of withdrawing financial support because program staff were never responsive to basic informational requests about their status and activities.

One of the supervisors suddenly had a breakthrough experience in the process of constructing the mission statement. She delivered an emotionally powerful speech about how important this program was to her, because it was one of the last social welfare programs remaining from the Johnson administration's War Against Poverty. The dialogue about the mission of this program brought her back to the roots of the program and reminded her why she had supported it in the first place. The staff members were stunned to learn the depth of her commitment to the program during this workshop. The mission became a vehicle to reconnect to the program and to the values associated with this effort. It also served to establish a link between the formerly alienated and antagonistic parties. The supervisor/funder commented afterward that the experience of empowerment evaluation was both powerful and tricky, and it forced her to return to her commitment to both the ideals of the program, as well as program practice itself. They generated the same kind of documents reported in earlier case examples. (See the Upward Bound Empowerment Evaluation Notes at the end of this chapter for examples of this program's mission statement as well as goals, strategies, and documentation.)

■ Summer School Program

The summer school case highlights the power of empowerment evaluation to raise fundamental issues about program design and implementation. Paul St. Roseman and I served as the empowerment evaluators. The college student program was designed to help middle school students improve their academic performance through classroom instruction and other enriching activities. Similar to the Upward Bound program dynamic, the summer school program staff members did not trust their supervisors and sponsors. The supervisors and sponsors were reaching the point of "writing this group off" because the staff were not responsive to suggestions to improve the program, their summer school students were unruly, and the program was expensive.

The process of generating a mission and taking stock of the program caused the student director of the program to raise fundamental questions about the existence of the program. She asked whether the program should continue to exist, whether it fit into the larger mission of the college, and if the director should be a professional full-time staff member instead of a student. The supervisors and sponsors were stunned. These were fundamental questions they had not been able to articulate in the last three years before this workshop. These discussions forced everyone to step back and allocate more time to a complete program redesign. This approach created an environment and mechanisms to facilitate this kind of fundamental change in program design and implementation. (See the Summer School Program Empowerment Evaluation notes at the end of this chapter for the mission and taking stock documents for this case study.)

■ Conclusion

The four case examples presented in this chapter help illustrate the strength and simplicity of this approach. In addition, a brief review of case examples helps set the stage for a more detailed examination of a high stakes empowerment evaluation—focusing on accreditation in higher education.

Upward Bound Empowerment Evaluation Notes

▪ Mission—Key Components

- To generate in low-income, potential first generation college students the skills and motivation necessary to complete a program of secondary education and to enter and complete a program of postsecondary education.
- To inform parents of the range of postsecondary educational opportunities available to their children, and to support and encourage their active involvement in the secondary and the postsecondary educational process.
- To educate youth, university students, and school systems about equal educational opportunity, and to advocate on behalf of program youth.
- To develop within university students the skills essential to teach and guide socioeconomically disadvantaged youth and to enrich their educational lives.
- To educate university students about the educational, social, political, economic, and racial issues that create the context for their work with Upward Bound youth and beyond.

▪ Key Activities/Elements

Mentoring

Goals:

- Maximize the learning benefit to both university students and Upward Bound students.
- Maximize the length of the mentoring relationship (so that the mentor/mentee want to remain together).
- Maximize the depth of the mentoring relationship.
- Maximize the receptivity of Upward Bound students to a mentoring relationship.[1]

Strategies: (What strategies would you like to use in order to achieve the goals?)

- Maximize tutor/tutee attendance.
- Improve training of university students—provide a framework for mentoring.
- Receptivity decreases because of a perceived instability in the relationship Ô Institute mentor contract.
- Internship credit for tutoring Ô Attendance becomes mandatory to the credit, including the reflection time for the university students. (Possibly a way to add accountability and commitment to the program?)

Documentation: (What already exists? What should be used? Are there ways to improve what is already in place? Existing data—What do you already have access to?)

- Attendance
- Tutor applications (add an end date so that length can be tracked)
- Employment contracts
- Grades and improvement of intermediate outcomes such as writing, study habits, etc. (Do improvements correlate with length of association with a particular tutor?)
- Matriculation reports
- Contact logs
- Surveys of Upward Bound students and staff following completion of programs
- Surveys after training programs
- Possible addition: surveys after workshops (short, one-page evaluation sheets on instructor, room, food, if they learned anything, etc.)

General Notes:

- Self-assessment brings credibility because there are opportunities to present both the good programs as well as the programs that need improvement.
- Keep in mind that it is important to track and document those activities that are being done well.
- What kind of longitudinal relationships already exist? What is it about these relationships that make it a lasting relationship? What is it about the long-

term relationships that made it into a richer experience than the average? What is the pattern?[2]

- Building a tracking system for alumnus ➔ Provide key examples of success (stories are powerful qualitative documentation, as well as numbers/states).

- The taking stock numbers and explanations provide a baseline for demonstrating change over time.

- Important strategy—document narratives as you go (rather than wait), institutionalize a space for this data—producing short reports, photos, and so forth.

Service Learning

Goals:

- To provide opportunities for all participants (Upward Bound and university students) to learn from reflecting on their experiences in the program.

- Continuity in service ➔ Specific strategies help provide continuity/an integrated approach.

- Communicate clearly what service learning is.

■ Notes

1. Implicit in the second and third goal is to encourage continuity.

2. These questions are geared toward generating ideas for tracking university students.

Summer School Program Empowerment Evaluation Notes

▓ Mission

List of Summer School Mission Items

- Enrich the lives of Summer School participants[1] (academically and socially).
- Instill in participants a desire to attend an institution of higher education.
- Prepare participants for academic and social adjustment to high school.
- Address broader social issues.
- Improve life skills and decision-making capacity.
- Summer School Program provides University students with professional development opportunities (motivates students to go into education or possibly nonprofit work).
- Collaborate with other organizations (like the Girls' Club).
- Summer School Program seeks a sustained relationship and commitment to its target community.
- Summer School Program provides mentors to its participants.
- Summer School Program provides participants a connection with other students in the community.
- The Parent Organization provides the Summer School Program staff with service learning for students who aspire to go into nonprofit/education work. (Possibly link with university's teacher education program).

Issues and Concerns

- Summer School Program 's Executive Director (ED) would like to see a stronger working relationship with the schools that Summer School Program participants attend. (The Associate Director indicates that the school sites would like this as well.)
- Summer School Program 's ED would like to provide more resources to the family (possibly via referral). Issues that Summer School Program encounters

include testing for learning disability and referral of non–Summer School Program youth to other programs (family referral services could connect to developing the working relationship with the school sites as indicated in the first bulleted item).

- Summer School Program staff would like to increase the number of participants who attend the program.

Mission Themes

- Summer School Program educational mission for its participants.
- The Parent Organization's academic and professional mission for university students.
- Collaboration with community.

Taking Stock (Phase I)—Summer School Program Activities That Address the Mission

Baseline[2]: Operational Items

- **Academic classes—[5 votes]—rank #2**
- **Workshop (around social issues)—[5 votes]—rank #3**
- Counselor elective (courses)
- Community service
- Job training
- **Test preparation (SAT and writing skills)—[4 votes]—rank #7**
- **School-year tutoring [5 votes]—rank #6**
- Field trips
- **Curriculum development (school year)—[3 votes]—rank #10**
- Participant recruitment
- Family socials
- **University student preparation and training for work with Summer School Program—[3 votes]—rank #9**
- Teaching electives (counselors)
- Home visits.
- **Service learning (Parent Organization coursework for university students)—[5 votes]—rank #4**
- Evaluation

- Provide training for university students
- **Fundraising (university students)—[4 votes]—rank #8**
- **Communication—[5 votes]—rank #5**
- **Train tutors—[5 votes]—rank #1**

■ Taking Stock (Phase II)—Summer School Program Staff and Sponsor/Administration Staff Rate the Top 10 Items

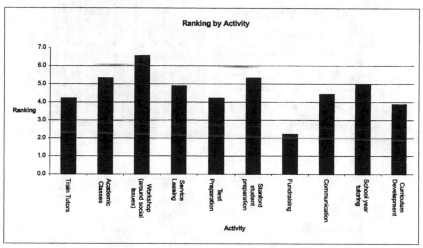

Figure 4.18. Graph #1, Ranking by Activity.

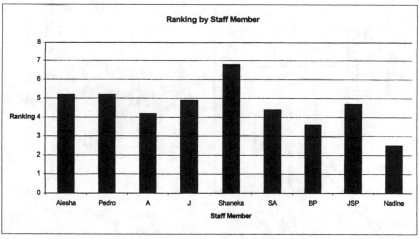

Figure 4.19. Graph #2, Ranking by Staff Member. (Cross reference with Figure 4.20—total average ranking by staff member.)

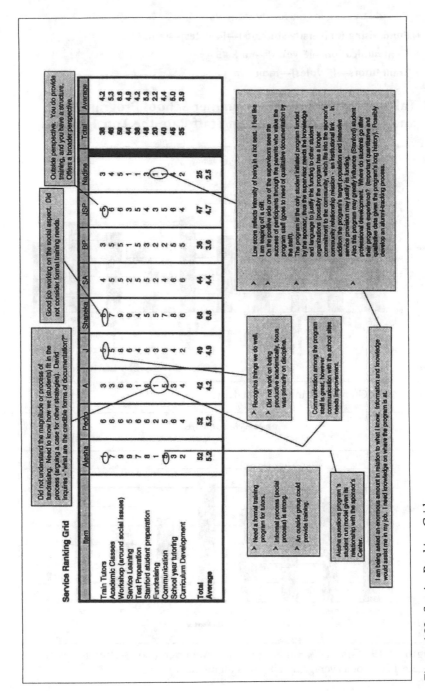

Figure 4.20. Service Ranking Grid.

▪ Notes

1. "Summer School Program participants" refer to middle school students who benefit from Summer School Program's academic and social enrichment services.

2. To establish a baseline, each staff member was instructed to select, in his or her opinion, the top 10 operational items. The number of votes each item received is provided, as is its final ranking.

▪ Notes

1. Storytelling is a form of debriefing after a key event. Staff members told stories about exhilarating and depressing experiences in the hospital as a way to share insights and lessons learned during staff meetings. It was a bonding event or tool.

2. "Caring Community Reads" is a pseudonym for the real program, which prefers to remain anonymous.

A HIGH-STAKES CASE EXAMPLE

Documenting the Utility,
Credibility, and Rigor of
Empowerment Evaluation
in a High-Stakes Arena—
Accreditation

Opportunity is missed by most people because it is
dressed in overalls, and looks like work.

—*Thomas Edison*

One measure of the power and credibility of an evaluative approach is the degree to which it is adopted in high-stakes assessments and forms of accountability. This discussion highlights a case in point, presenting a brief case study of empowerment evaluation as it has been adopted in an accreditation self-study. This accreditation study was considered a high-stakes event in higher education for all parties involved, including the accrediting agency.

■ The Institute: A Case Example

The California Institute of Integral Studies is an independent graduate school located in San Francisco. It has been accredited since 1981 by the Western Association of Schools and Colleges (WASC) of the Commission for Senior Colleges and Universities of Schools and Colleges. The accreditation process requires periodic self-evaluations. The Institute adopted an empowerment evaluation approach as a tool to institutionalize evaluation as part of the planning and management of operations and to respond to the accreditation self-study requirement. The evaluation had three parts: The first stage focused on identifying the program mission; the second, taking stock, examined and assessed the merit of a unit, and the third part was designed to establish goals and strategies to improve program practice. In addition, in this final stage evidence was specified to monitor change over time. This third stage was part of strategic planning and was built on the collaborative foundation of understanding informed by mission and taking stock activities.

All units in the Institute—including academic, governance, and administrative units—conducted self-evaluations. The purpose of these evaluations was to improve operations and build a base for planning and decision making. In addition to focusing on improvement, these self-evaluations contributed to institutional accountability.

Workshops were conducted throughout the Institute to provide training in evaluation techniques and procedures. All unit heads attended the training sessions, which were held over three days. They then served as facilitators in their own groups. Training and individual technical assistance was also provided throughout the year for governance and other administrative groups, including the Office of the President and the Development Office. (See the empowerment evaluation notes on the California Institute of Integral Studies at the end of this chapter for additional detail.)

The self-evaluation process required thoughtful reflection and inquiry. The units described their purpose and listed approximately 10 key activities that characterized their unit. Members of the unit democratically determined the top 10 activities that merited consideration and evaluation. Then each member of a unit evaluated each activity by rating the activities on a 1 (*low*) to 10 (*high*) scale. Individual ratings were combined to produce a group or unit rating for each activity and one for the total unit. Unit members then reviewed these ratings. A sample matrix is provided in Figure 5.1 to illustrate how this process was implemented.

STL Wide Self-Evaluation Worksheet (Subpopulation Sample for Demonstration)													
Activities	EK	KK	YT	DE	BH	MT	EG	DF	JA	MC		Subtl	Average
1 Building Capacity	7	5	7	5	5	5	7	5	6	8		62	6.2
2 Teaching	5	6	8	8	6	8	8	8	8	9		74	7.4
3 Research	5	7	7	3	6	6	3	7	7	6		58	5.8
4 Transformative Learning	8	6	6	5	5	7	9	7	7	8		68	6.8
5 Dissemination - scholarly	3	6	7	4	6	6	5	8	5	5		55	5.5
6 Enhance health relationship ClIS	7	8	8	6	6	8	5	7	5	7		65	6.5
7 Community Building	6	6	7	6	7	7	6	6	6	8		65	6.5
8 Curriculum dev/refin/eval	8	6	7	7	7	7	8	8	8	8		74	7.4
9 Experimental pedagogy	8	6	9	8	8	8	8	8	8	9		80	8
10 Diversity	5	4	8	6	5	7	5	4	4	6		54	5.4
Subtotal	62	58	74	58	61	71	62	70	65	74	655	655	65.5 Subtotal
												65.5	Average (activity)
Average	6.2	5.8	7.4	5.8	6.1	7.1	6.2	7	6.5	7.4	65.5	6.55	Average (person)
												6.55	Unit Average

Figure 5.1. Sample Self-Evaluation Worksheet. This matrix was used in an empowerment evaluation session for the California Institute of Integral Studies, and is a sample of a subpopulation for demonstration purposes. *STL*, in the top line, stands for the name of one of the Institute schools: School for Transformative Learning. On the left is an abbreviated list of critical activities associated with the School. In the middle of the matrix are initials of members of the school (e.g., EK, KK, YT), under which are the person's ratings concerning the activities listed on the left side of the matrix. Each person's rating is totaled on the right side under *Subtl.* Then each subtotal is averaged at the far right of the matrix. Similarly, each individual's ratings are totaled and averaged to determine who is optimistic and pessimistic in the group, and to facilitate the norming process within the group. At the far right bottom of the matrix is the average of the scores (both for the activities and for each individual) to create an overall unit or program average. Program participants are more likely to give a realistic overall average after being given the opportunity to state where they are doing well and where they are not doing as well concerning program performance.

77

Unit members discussed and dissected the meaning of the activities listed in the matrix and the ratings given to each activity. This exchange provided unit members with an opportunity to establish norms concerning the meaning of terms and ratings in an open and collegial atmosphere. Unit members were also required to provide evidence or documentation for each rating and/or to identify areas in which additional documentation was needed. These self-evaluations represented the first baseline data about program and unit operations concerning the entire Institute. This process was superior to survey methods for four reasons. First, unit members determined what to focus on to improve their own programs—improving the validity of the effort and the buy-in required to implement recommendations. Second, a majority of members of the community were immersed in the evaluation experience, making the process of building a culture of evidence and a community of learners as important as the specific evaluative outcomes. Third, members of the community entered into a dialogue about the ratings helping them establish norms and common understandings. Finally, there was a 100% return rate, as compared with typically low return rates for surveys.

These self-evaluations were used to implement specific improvements in program practice. This process was used to reexamine and reframe existing problems, leading to solutions, adaptations, and new activities for the future. It was also used to reframe existing data from traditional sources, enabling participants to give meaningful interpretation to data they already collect. In addition, self-evaluations were used to ensure programmatic and academic accountability. For example, the Psychology program decided to discontinue its Ph.D. program as part of the self-evaluation process—a significant measure of internal or external accountability. The viability of the program had been a significant WASC and Institute concern of long standing. The core of the problem was that there were not enough faculty members to properly serve the number of matriculating students in their program. The empowerment evaluation process provided a vehicle for the faculty to come to terms with this problem in an open, self-conscious manner. The faculty had complained about the work load and working conditions before, but they had never consciously analyzed, diagnosed, and documented this problem because they did not have the time or a simple, nonthreatening mechanism to assess themselves. They were dedicated to serving students properly, but when they analyzed faculty-to-student ratios and faculty dissertation loads, the problem became self-evident. Empowerment evaluation provided Institute faculty with a tool to evaluate the program in light of scarce resources and make an executive decision to discontinue the program. Similarly, one of the Institute's on-line Ph.D. programs was administratively merged with another distance learning program as a result of this self-evaluative process. This was done to provide greater efficiencies of scale, improve monitoring and supervision, and provide more face-to-face contact with the Institute. (For a description of one of these on-line educational programs, see Fetterman, 1996b, 1996c.)

The last stage of the empowerment evaluation involved building plans for the future based on these evaluations. All units at the Institute completed their plans for the future, and these data were used to design an overall strategic plan. Goals and strategies were specified. In addition, relevant evidence was specified to monitor progress toward selected goals. This process ensured community involvement and commitment to the effort, generating a plan that was grounded in the reality of unit practice. The Provost institutionalized this process by requiring self-evaluations and unit plans on an annual basis to facilitate program improvement and contribute to institutional accountability.

■ Conclusion

The match between empowerment evaluation and accreditation self-study requirements was strong and productive. There are many user-friendly tools designed to help participants make credible judgments about where they are at any given point in time; identify consistent patterns of behavior that are meaningful to the group; facilitate comparison— across individuals, categories, and programs; and stimulate constructive activity to improve program practice. For example, a matrix or spreadsheet was used here to highlight the empowerment evaluation process at the Institute. This tool further systematized internal evaluation activity and facilitated comparison and analysis on a larger scale.[1]

In this empowerment evaluation design, developed in response to a school's accreditation self-study requirement, a series of external evaluations were planned to build on and enhance self-evaluation efforts. A series of external teams were invited to review specific programs. They determined the evaluation agenda in conjunction with department faculty, staff, and students. However, they operated as critical friends providing a strategic consultation rather than a compliance or traditional accountability review. Although an external evaluation is not a requirement of empowerment evaluation, this combination of forces highlights how empowerment evaluation and traditional external evaluation are not mutually exclusive, despite empowerment evaluation's focus on self-determination and collaboration. In fact, they enhance each other. The empowerment evaluation process produces a rich data source that enables a more complete external examination. Concurrently, external evaluators can also help determine the merit and worth of various activities. Participants agreed on the value of an external perspective to add insights into program operation, serve as an additional quality control, sharpen inquiry, and improve program practice. Greater coordination between the needs of the internal and external forms of evaluation can provide a reality check concerning external needs and expectations for insiders, and a rich database for external evaluators.

Finally, it is hoped that empowerment evaluation will continue to benefit from the artful shaping of our combined contributions, both internally or externally, rather than follow any single approach or strategy. As Cronbach (1980) urged over a decade ago, "It is better for an evaluative inquiry to launch a small fleet of studies than to put all its resources into a single approach" (p. 7).

This high-stakes case example, in conjunction with the case examples discussed earlier in Chapter 4, further documents the utility and rigor of this approach. These examples also set the stage for a discussion about empowerment evaluation and evaluation standards. The case examples were primarily presented to highlight the steps and the power of this approach; however, they also indicate how this approach meets and often exceeds evaluation standards. A methodical and systematic examination of how empowerment evaluation meets the standards is presented in the next chapter to extend this discussion in an explicit manner.

California Institute of Integral Studies Empowerment Evaluation Notes

■ 1994–1995 Unit Self-Evaluation Workshops for Unit Heads

Times and Places

February 7, 4:00–6:00, 4th floor Conference Room.

February 9, 4:00–6:00, 4th floor Conference Room.

February 12, 12:00–2:00, All Saint's Church.

Workshop Facilitators

David Fetterman, Karine Schomer, and Mary Curran.

Agenda

1. Introduction
   - Purpose of the unit self-evaluation: How it will feed into the academic program review and the WASC self-study
   - Unit-based strategic planning
2. Timelines and deadlines, report formats
3. The Self-Empowerment Evaluation Method: Purpose, process, and product
4. Overarching Institute and WASC issues and themes
5. Conducting a demonstration taking stock session with a volunteer unit

Part I

1. Volunteer unit members describe their unit, its mission or purpose, and its relationship to the Institute's mission.

2. They list the unit's key activities.

3. They rate the quality and/or effectiveness of the top ten key activities.

4. They list documentation and evidence to support the ratings.

5. They do an overall rating of the unit.

Part II: Break-Out Period

1. Volunteer unit members discuss among themselves their ratings of key activities: Why did each person rate as he/she did? What did the ratings mean to each person? How did the unit achieve the rating given? How could it achieve a higher rating? Should ratings be adjusted in view of the discussion?

2. Meanwhile, other workshop participants form small groups. Each person writes a description of their unit, lists five key activities, rates these activities and the unit as a whole, and lists supporting documentation. Then all this is reported and discussed in the group.

3. Small group discussions are shared in the large group.

Part III

1. Volunteer group adjusts its ratings of the unit's key activities.

2. They adjust their overall rating of the unit.

3. They prioritize the key activities they have rated.

4. They list two to three preliminary recommendations for future courses of action: major goals, objectives related to the goals, strategies to achieve the objectives, documentation/evidence that would demonstrate success.

Instructions for Unit Tasks After
Completion of the Taking Stock Session

1. Unit head writes up a preliminary Unit Self-Evaluation Report based on the taking stock session, including the unit mission/purpose, overall unit rating, rating of key activities, prioritization of key activities, list of documentation/evidence to support ratings, and preliminary recommendations for future courses of action.

2. Mini-sessions of the unit are held to review the report, discuss and adjust ratings, and build consensus about what the ratings mean and what everyone thinks about the unit.

3. Supporting documentation is gathered and analyzed.

4. Unit head completes and submits final draft of the Unit Self-Evaluation Report and supporting documentation.

■ 1994–1995 Unit Self-Evaluation Report Instructions

Note 1: The report form is available on disk from the Office of the Provost. (Please supply your own disk.)

Note 2: A single report format is being used for academic, administrative, and governance units. Some items may therefore not be applicable to all units. They should be marked *N/A*.

Note 3: Reports and supporting documentation should be reviewed by person whom unit head reports to before submission to Office of the Provost.

Note 4: Reports should be distributed as widely as possible within each unit and to other relevant units.

Name of Unit: _____

What larger unit does it belong to? _____

Academic/Administrative/Governance (circle one)

Name and title of unit head: _____

To whom does unit head report? (Title): _____

Part I: Unit Description

1. Mission or purpose of the unit (narrative)

2. Relationship to the Institute's mission

3. Organizational structure of the unit (narrative)

4. List of ten (10) key activities performed by the unit, prioritized (from the taking stock session)

5. Other ongoing activities of the unit (narrative)

6. Special projects of the unit (list)

7. Direction of the unit development over the past three years (narrative)

8. Current three (3) major goals, objectives related to goals, strategies being used to achieve objectives, and documentation or evidence that demonstrates success (narrative)

9. Number and names of core faculty by % time

10. Number and names of adjunct faculty

11. Number and names of staff, by title and % time

12. Number of students (estimated persons over the past three years: 1992–1993, 1993–1994, and 1994–1995)

13. Number of students (full time equivalent) over the past three years: 1992–1993, 1993–1994, and 1994–1995 (estimated)

14. Number of class enrollments over the past three years: 1992–1993, 1993–1994, and 1994–1995 (estimated)

15. Operational budget for the past two years and current year: 1992–1993, 1993–1994, and 1994–1995

   Revenue Expense (Note: Please footnote any figures requiring significant explanation.)

16. Institutional issues and themes of particular relevance to the unit (refer to the Strategic Directions document provided ealier)

17. WASC issues and themes of particular relevance to the unit (refer to WASC recommendations, WASC Standards, and WASC Self-Study Themes)

Part II: Unit Self-Evaluation

1. Names of participants in the unit self-evaluation process
   (F = faculty, S = student, AS = administrative staff)

2. Date(s) of the taking stock session(s)

3. Dates and purpose of the follow-up mini-sessions

4. Narrative of the self-evaluation process

5. Overall rating of the unit

   Range: _____

   Average: _____

6. Rating of prioritized 10 key activities (list)

Item	Range	Average
(1)		
(2)		
(3)		
(4)		
(5)		
(6)		
(7)		
(8)		
(9)		
(10)		

7. List of documentation or evidence used to support ratings (attach documentation in appendix)

8. Discussion of findings (narrative based on overall ratings and ratings of prioritized ten key activities). Describe the key activities and how they are related to the mission or purpose of the unit. Explain what the individual and overall ratings mean. Explain the relevance of the documentation used. Summarize the overall strengths and weaknesses of the unit and progress made over the past three years.

9. Preliminary recommendations for two to three future courses of actions: major new goals, objectives related to the goals, strategies to achieve the objectives, and documentation or evidence that would demonstrate success.

10. Evaluation and feedback on the unit self-evaluation process

■ Notes

1. Another technique involves a more artistic approach using green and red dots to signify, respectively, progress or problems concerning specific program activities. The dots have a strong visual impact, and can be easily quantified.

6

THE STANDARDS

Applying the Standards
to Empowerment Evaluation

Man's reach should exceed his grasp, or what's a
heaven for?

—Robert Browning

Standards are designed to ensure a measure of quality in our work. They also serve to unify a profession with a common language and set of values. They are not and should not be carved in stone for all time; however, they typically reflect the status quo in a given field or profession, and as such provide a useful reference point from that perspective. The standards for program evaluation, as such, represent a useful tool for self-reflection and examination.[1] Applying the standards to empowerment evaluation (a) documents how this approach meets the standards and (b) improves and refines empowerment evaluation in the process. This exercise also forces us to reexamine the value and applicability of the standards. This

87

chapter discusses specifically how empowerment evaluation meets or exceeds the spirit of the standards in terms of utility, feasibility, propriety, and
accuracy.

■ Utility Standards

Utility standards are intended to ensure that an evaluation will serve the
information needs of intended users. They are, according to the Joint
Committee on Standards for Educational Evaluation (1994),

U1. *Stakeholder Identification.* Persons involved in or affected by the evaluation should be identified, so that their needs can be addressed.

U2. *Evaluator Credibility.* The persons conducting the evaluation should
be both trustworthy and competent to perform the evaluation, so that
the evaluation findings achieve maximum credibility and acceptance.

U3. *Information Scope and Selection.* Information collected should be
broadly selected to address pertinent questions about the program
and be responsive to the needs and interests of clients and other specified stakeholders.

U4. *Values Identification.* The perspectives, procedures, and rationale used
to interpret the findings should be carefully described, so that the
bases for value judgments are clear.

U5. *Report Clarity.* Evaluation reports should clearly describe the program
being evaluated, including its context, and the purposes, procedures,
and findings of the evaluation, so that essential information is provided and easily understood.

U6. *Report Timeliness and Dissemination.* Significant interim findings and
evaluation reports should be disseminated to intended users, so that
they can be used in a timely fashion.

U7. *Evaluation Impact.* Evaluations should be planned, conducted, and reported in ways that encourage follow-through by stakeholders, so
that the likelihood that the evaluation will be used is increased.

Empowerment evaluation requires the involvement of as many people
involved in or affected by the evaluation as possible so that their needs can
be addressed. The group evaluates its own program, with the help of facili-

tators (members of the group being evaluated) and coaches (such as external or internal experts in evaluation) who provide assistance in the design and execution of the (often iterative) evaluation plan. Coaches can also provide workshops and other forms of training to ensure capacity building. Empowerment evaluation is an open, democratic, group process. Trustworthiness is enhanced as a function of group participation—everyone is given a chance to be heard, and plans are routinely adjusted to accommodate a member's concerns, including conflicting views and minority reports. In addition, members of the group are responsible for every stage of the evaluation, from planning to reporting findings and recommendations.

All participants provide information about key program elements and concerns. For example, in the empowerment evaluation of the graduate school program discussed in Chapter 5, faculty, staff, students, and administrators were directly involved in the process at every stage. They listed and prioritized pertinent questions about the program. In addition, the concerns and perspectives of external bodies, such as an accreditation agency, were also solicited. In fact, the accreditation agency's standards and previous critiques of the program served as a powerful context within which to construct an empowerment evaluation. Program participants focused on perspectives, procedures, and the rationale for interpreting findings during the planning stage and throughout the evaluation. As new knowledge and/or insights emerge and are fed back into the program, evaluation processes and procedures may need to be retooled and refined. Their continuing participation increases the likelihood that members will accept and internalize the bases for value judgments. However, because people change (often as a result of this experience), the group must revisit its value judgments at various junctures throughout the process—in some instances a lifelong process.

The proposals and reports generated from an empowerment evaluation typically describe the program being evaluated, including its context and purposes, procedures, and findings of the evaluation. Interim communications are routine in empowerment evaluation; they serve to take the pulse of the group at critical phases in its daily operation. Not all forms of communication require a reiteration of the program description and procedures, however; for example, as a member of one group using empowerment evaluation, I used a "burnout thermometer" to take the pulse of other program participants who were complaining about job burnout. Everyone was asked to mark their level of burnout on a thermometer drawn on a poster board. It proved to be a powerful visual display of the group's feelings of being depleted by work overload and job stress at that point in time. It also provided a baseline for comparison with perceptions throughout the year. In addition to traditional memoranda and reports, this form of data provided rapid turn-around of information, insights, and interpretations, enabling participants to use the information in a timely manner. All information generated is designed to be fed back into the system to encourage follow-through by stakeholders. This often requires presenting the same information more than once and in multiple forms. Peer pressure is a powerful force in holding people accountable for what they have or have not done with the evaluation findings and recommendations. The process of encouraging follow-through is also greatly facilitated by existing governance structures or hierarchy, both formal and informal.

■ Feasibility Standards

Feasibility standards are intended to ensure that an evaluation will be realistic, prudent, diplomatic, and frugal. They are as follows:

F1. *Practical Procedures.* The evaluation procedures should be practical, to keep disruption to a minimum while needed information is obtained.

F2. *Political Viability.* The evaluation should be planned and conducted with anticipation of the different positions of various interest groups, so that their cooperation may be obtained, and so that possible attempts by any of these groups to curtail evaluation operations or to bias or misapply the results can be averted or counteracted.

F3. *Cost Effectiveness.* The evaluation should be efficient and produce information of sufficient value, so that the resources expended can be justified. (Joint Committee on Standards for Educational Evaluation, 1994)

Empowerment evaluation is a practical approach to evaluation. Program participants are encouraged to use existing databases and tools, rather than reinvent the wheel. For example, most programs maintain budget information, attendance, and attrition records. These forms of information are invaluable in any evaluation; there is no need to create a new mechanism to capture these data. This approach keeps disruption to a minimum. However, empowerment evaluation also requires program-level introspection and norming concerning how individuals rate program elements—initially a time consuming process. Self-evaluation can seem deceptively simple and non-intrusive if this up-front effort is overlooked. It is an invaluable investment, however, because the norming process helps build a foundation of understanding about what program participants concerns are and how they define a high or low rating.

Empowerment evaluation by the group or program means that most viewpoints are represented, including radically divergent points of views and values. Involvement by as many people as possible from each stratum or interest group minimizes but does not eliminate the power of any specific group to shape or bias the evaluation effort. However, this open process greatly reduces the likelihood that any subgroup will attempt to curtail evaluation operations, especially senior management. In fact, the group buy-in associated with this approach makes it virtually impossible for senior management to curtail it, once initiated. In addition, a lengthy audit trail documents the process and procedures. Cooperation (or, more accurately negotiation) is the norm in empowerment evaluations. This evaluation approach is efficient because it relies on existing resources and provides invaluable information routinely, ranging from the credibility and accuracy of budget projections to the degree of success in achieving the group's intended outcome and impact.

■ Propriety Standards

Propriety standards are intended to ensure that an evaluation will be conducted legally, ethically, and with due regard for the welfare of those involved in the evaluation, as well as those affected by its results. These standards are

P1. *Service Orientation.* Evaluations should be designed to assist organizations to address and effectively serve the needs of the full range of targeted participants.

P2. *Formal Agreements.* Obligations of the formal parties to an evaluation (i.e., what is to be done, how, by whom, and when) should be agreed to in writing, so that these parties are obligated to adhere to all conditions of the agreement or formally to renegotiate it.

P3. *Rights of Human Subjects.* Evaluations should be designed and conducted to respect and protect the rights and welfare of human subjects.

P4. *Human Interactions.* Evaluators should respect human dignity and worth in their interactions with other persons associated with an evaluation, so that participants are not threatened or harmed.

P5. *Complete and Fair Assessment.* The evaluation should be complete and fair in its examination and recording of strengths and weaknesses of the program being evaluated, so that strengths can be built upon and problem areas addressed.

P6. *Disclosure of Findings.* The formal parties to an evaluation should ensure that the full set of evaluation findings along with pertinent limitations are made accessible to the persons affected by the evaluation, and any others with expressed legal rights to receive the results.

P7. *Conflict of Interest.* Conflict of interest should be dealt with openly and honestly, so that it does not compromise the evaluation processes and results.

P8. *Fiscal Responsibility.* The evaluator's allocation and expenditure of resources should reflect sound accountability procedures and otherwise be prudent and ethically responsible, so that expenditures are accounted for and appropriate. (Joint Committee on Standards for Educational Evaluation, 1994)

By their nature and the requirement of group involvement, empowerment evaluations are designed to be service oriented, assisting organizations as they address and effectively serve the needs of the full range of targeted participants. Formal agreements exist in empowerment evaluation; however, they are necessarily different from those in the standards, which are designed for individual external evaluators. In empowerment evaluation, the group creates its own agreements—often in writing or in job descriptions—concerning the evaluation plan, specific procedures, responsibilities of participants for the various components of the self-evaluation, and a timeline. These elements are open to renegotiation as priorities and people change. Empowerment evaluations are designed and conducted in a manner that respects and protects the rights and welfare of human beings. In one such effort, a formal human subjects committee approval process was deemed appropriate and an informed consent document was generated and disseminated.

Empowerment evaluations are grounded in a profound respect for human dignity and worth. In fact, this respect is the basis for encouraging program participants to take charge of their own lives using evaluation as one tool. Every effort is taken to ensure that program participants do not threaten, undermine, or harm each other. However, empowerment evaluations are extremely self-critical. The process of reflection and dialogue associated with empowerment evaluation can be quite difficult and routinely uncomfortable. Basic assumptions—never mind preliminary findings—are questioned at almost every meeting. In this regard, the process can be threatening. Ideally, an atmosphere of trust is created to facilitate open and honest self-critique. Periodically, additional precautions and reminders are needed to maintain a secure, safe environment, free from emotional or intellectual "cannibalism."

Empowerment evaluations are thorough[2] and fair. Everyone has an opportunity to identify and engage each of the issues. In addition, there are no topics too sacred to address; typically, the most sacred, unspoken concerns emerge as the highest priority items. Documentation is always required to support a high or low rating about a program assessment, and is scrutinized. Precision is important; however, it is second to usefulness. Both strengths and weakness are evaluated in order to build on strengths and improve areas of concern.

Empowerment evaluation is not exhaustive. Documents and views are examined as completely as possible, given time and resources. Concerns are prioritized and reprioritized routinely by the group to adjust and be responsive to program priorities. Items routinely placed on the bottom of the list are flagged, and a task force is convened to respond to the items and reflect on why they have been routinely listed as less significant than other concerns. The task force is also responsible for making recommendations to the group concerning its findings. Many of these findings and recommendations can be easily understood and implemented. Systemic findings, however, are considered and acted on by the group as a whole.

All members of a group or program are entitled to a full set of findings and recommendations, as well as most interim communications. Some communications have a limited distribution list because they are designed to test a hypothesis or place a check on a preliminary interpretation or finding. Once closure is reached on a specific topic, such communications are more broadly disseminated. Similarly, there are some personal and personnel issues that do not receive full disclosure to respect the privacy of individuals.

Conflict of interest is a high priority in empowerment or self-evaluations, and is guarded against carefully. In one project, a member of a distance learning group was also the owner of the electronic communications system used by the program. The conflict of interest was discussed and debated, particularly because complaints about the program were reframed by the owner of the electronic communications system as the group's problem or fault—instead of being considered a design flaw or problem. In other words, his dual role made him unresponsive to the group's concerns. The group, including this individual, agreed that it was necessary for him to excuse himself from certain decisions about the program. Avenues were made available for continued discourse, but decisions were kept at arms' length. This was a direct result of a self-evaluative and reflective process.

The group is responsible for any allocation or expenditure of resources—primarily their own time. All discussions and decisions, including the allocation of resources, are typically open to all parties involved. The standard, once again, was written from a different frame of reference; however, the emphasis on sound accountability procedures, as well as prudent and ethically responsible fiscal behavior, is a useful reminder.

■ Accuracy Standards

The accuracy standards are intended to ensure that an evaluation will reveal and convey technically adequate information about the features that determine worth or merit of the program being evaluated. Accuracy standards are as follows:

- A1. *Program Documentation.* The program being evaluated should be described and documented clearly and accurately, so that the program is clearly identified.

- A2. *Context Analysis.* The context in which the program exists should be examined in enough detail, so that its likely influences on the program can be identified.

- A3. *Described Purposes and Procedures.* The purposes and procedures of the evaluation should be monitored and described in enough detail, so that they can be identified and assessed.

A4. *Defensible Information Sources.* The sources of information used in a program evaluation should be described in enough detail, so that the adequacy of the information can be assessed.

A5. *Valid Information.* The information-gathering procedures should be chosen or developed and then implemented so that they will assure that the interpretation arrived at is valid for the intended use.

A6. *Reliable Information.* The information-gathering procedures should be chosen or developed and then implemented so that they will assure that the information obtained is sufficiently reliable for the intended use.

A7. *Systematic Information.* The information collected, processed, and reported in an evaluation should be systematically reviewed and any errors found should be corrected.

A8. *Analysis of Quantitative Information.* Quantitative information in an evaluation should be appropriately and systematically analyzed so that evaluation questions are effectively answered.

A9. *Analysis of Qualitative Information.* Qualitative information in an evaluation should be appropriately and systematically analyzed so that evaluation questions are effectively answered.

A10. *Justified Conclusions.* The conclusions reached in an evaluation should be explicitly justified, so that stakeholders can assess them.

A11. *Impartial Reporting.* Reporting procedures should guard against distortion caused by personal feelings and biases of any party to the evaluation, so that evaluation reports fairly reflect the evaluation findings.

A12. *Metaevaluation.* The evaluation itself should be formatively and summatively evaluated against these and other pertinent standards, so that its conduct is appropriately guided and, on completion, stakeholders can closely examine its strengths and weaknesses. (Joint Committee on Standards for Educational Evaluation, 1994)

Empowerment evaluation uses a program description as both an exercise in defining where program participants are and where they would like to go in the future. It also serves as a baseline to measure change over time. For this purpose, the same description associated with report clarity in the utility standards is used in initial proposals and reports about the program. However, program descriptions are often altered during an empowerment evaluation, reflecting new aspirations and directions based on the formative feedback received from the process. A concerted effort is made to describe the unfolding process of how a program defines itself as it responds to new environmental constraints and new populations. In some cases, the initial definition is included in reports as part of the historical development of a program, providing a useful guide to the evolution of the program while remaining faithful to its newly developed identity. Slavishly adhering to a program definition that is no longer relevant would produce a mismatch and a misevaluation.

This does not mean that a program is never accountable. A self-evaluation is in the best position to document the process of such changes. Autocratic or whimsical changes that do not reflect planning and evaluation of program conditions, markets, consumers, and participants are reported in self-evaluations.

Context is critical in empowerment evaluation. The developmental life cycle of a program, for example, is highlighted. New programs are not held to the same evaluative standard as mature programs. Environmental conditions, as well as political, economic, and cultural factors, are considered paramount in self-evaluations. Contextualization enables program participants to interpret data meaningfully and to anticipate specific influences on program operation. Programs do not exist in a vacuum. The expectation that a program should break even financially in its second year of operation is a significant contextual variable that will shape program behavior during the first year. Similarly, violence, unemployment, and hunger are significant contextual variables in an inner city or a township, adding another dimension (and certainly an added degree of difficulty) to the development and operation of any program.

Empowerment evaluations, like many participatory forms of evaluation, are typically described in some detail. In fact the purposes and procedures often need to be repeated at various junctures because of turnover, procrastination, and the need for a refresher. A selected member of the group or a team of individuals develop and share an evaluation schedule. The process and flow of events are monitored by the group (and the facilitators). Significant milestones are celebrated and critiqued throughout the evaluation.

Empowerment evaluation workshops highlight the significance of defensible information sources. Program participants are always asked to provide documentation or evidence to support any rating. As discussed earlier, a participant who rates leadership a 3 on a 10-point scale, in which 10 is high, is challenged to provide evidence in two directions: first, to provide evidence to substantiate a low rating, and then to provide documentation to support a 3 rating instead of a 1 or 2. This process of challenging coworkers concerning defensible information continues throughout the effort. After a certain period of time, some sources become routinely acceptable. However, even the most basic sources can be challenged at any time.

The same process that is applied to securing defensible information sources is applied to securing valid and reliable information. This process often requires much soul searching when groups have significantly varying backgrounds. However, commonsense ground rules are usually established concerning information-gathering procedures.

Teams responsible for collecting, processing, and reporting systematically review their information. In addition, everyone has the opportunity to challenge any phase of the effort. When errors are found, they are corrected as quickly as possible. Data are rarely viewed as quantitative and qualitative in most empowerment evaluations: They are simply data. Data may be numerical or statistical as easily as narrative and descriptive. Program participants focus on the quality of the data, as well as issues of authenticity and trustworthiness. Qualitative and quantitative distinctions are generally left to the academics.

Conclusions need to be justified at every turn in an empowerment evaluation, and stakeholders are typically a vocal and highly critical part of the process. Positive and negative findings are equally challenged as either self-congratulatory or cynical. In either case, examples are requested, procedures reexamined, and conclusions either revised or their limitations noted.

Reporting procedures invite, rather than guard against, personal feelings and biases. Empowerment evaluation records the multicultural, pluralistic, human condition of any group or program. These elements of human life are considered vital to understanding how a program is working. They are not left out simply because they may contaminate or distort, or because they cannot easily be quantified. These factors are taken into consideration and reported to guard against distortion or omission, to ensure evaluation reports fairly reflect the evaluation findings. It is a radically different approach to accomplishing the same objective stated in the standard concerning impartial reporting.

Empowerment evaluations are often reviewed and evaluated. No program is free from external pressure or review. In one case, an accreditation agency served as the metaevaluator, reviewing and critiquing the self-evaluation plan. In another example, the program sponsor required an external examination and review of the evaluation plan and execution. In an inner-city school self-evaluation, the superintendent hired an external evaluator to review and evaluate the self-evaluation process and findings. However, not all programs have the time or resources to conduct a metaevaluation. Many programs run on a shoestring budget and adopt an empowerment evaluation because they do not have the resources to hire external evaluators. A metaevaluation becomes an unreasonable burden in those cases. (*Pro bono* efforts and exchanges of services have been used in some cases to accommodate these economic factors; e.g., one external peer group or team evaluates a program in exchange for a similar review of another program in their organization.)

Typically, the standards would be applied to an individual evaluation effort—whether an empowerment evaluation or another approach. However, applying the standards to empowerment evaluation in general is a useful exercise. It helps to elucidate many facets about the approach and provides some insight into the strengths and weakness of the standards themselves.

■ Conclusion

Empowerment evaluation is consistent with the spirit of the standards developed by the Joint Committee on Standards for Educational Evaluation (1994), including utility, feasibility, propriety, and accuracy standards, as well as the standard concerning impartial reporting. The application of the standards to empowerment evaluation help to illuminate many facets of this approach within a context shared or understood by many evaluators.

This chapter was presented in the best spirit of empowerment evaluation, which attempts to be accurate, responsive, honest, useful, and self-critical. The next chapter builds on this self-critical posture, by openly and self-consciously presenting caveats and concerns about empowerment evaluation.

■ Notes

1. There are many problems with the standards and the application of the standards to empowerment evaluation. In addition, they have not been formally adopted by any professional organization. However, they are at present the *de facto* standards in the field.

2. The term *thorough* is somewhat vague. Empowerment evaluation, like much sponsored evaluation, is pragmatic. A sincere effort is made to be thorough, but program participants have other things to do and typically apply the law of diminishing returns to any inquiry. Because any facet of the evaluation can be reevaluated (and often is) in an empowerment evaluation, a mechanism exists to ensure thoroughness on critical issues. The issue of compliance to a thoroughness standard should, however, raise a flag for any practitioner concerning the need to get the job done in a professional manner and keep within a budget. The question is often, What is realistic and practical, given the time and resources available? In addition, who will determine if the standard has been met, given real-world constraints?

CAVEATS

Discussing Caveats
and Concerns About
Empowerment Evaluation

We should not let our fears hold us back from pursuing
our hopes.

John F. Kennedy

Empowerment evaluation is not a panacea. It is one effective approach among many in the field. In addition, there are many legitimate questions raised in the use of empowerment evaluation that merit discussion and exploration. Questions about rigor, empowerment evaluation's relationship to traditional evaluation, objectivity, and bias are briefly discussed in this chapter. In addition, this chapter concludes with an exploration into the issue of privilege.

■ Rigor

Is research rigor maintained in empowerment evaluation? The case examples and the discussion about empowerment evaluation and the standards presented in this book illustrate how rigor in research and evaluation is maintained. Mechanisms employed to provide rigor included workshops and training; democratic participation in the evaluation to ensure that majority and minority views are represented; quantifiable rating matrices to create a baseline measure of progress; discussion and definition of terms and ratings (i.e., norming); scrutinizing documentation; and questioning findings and recommendations. These mechanisms, among others, help ensure that program participants are critical, analytical, and honest.

Empowerment evaluation is one approach among many being used to address social, educational, industrial, health care, and many other problems. As with the exploration and development of any new frontier, this approach requires adaptations, alterations, and innovations. This does not, however, mean that significant compromises must be made in the rigor required to conduct evaluations. Although I am a major proponent of individuals taking evaluation into their own hands and conducting self-evaluations, I recognize the need for adequate research, preparation, and planning. These first discussions need to be supplemented with reports, texts, workshops, classroom instruction, and apprenticeship experiences if possible. Program personnel new to evaluation should seek the assistance of an evaluator to act as coach, assisting in the design and execution of an evaluation. Furthermore, an evaluator must be judicious in determining when it is appropriate to function as an empowerment evaluator or in any other evaluative role.

■ Traditional Evaluation

Does empowerment evaluation abolish traditional evaluation? New approaches require a balanced assessment. A strict constructionist perspective may strangle a young enterprise; too liberal a stance is certain to transform a novel tool into another fad. Colleagues who fear that we are giving evaluation away are right in one respect: We are sharing it with a much broader population. But those who fear that we are educating ourselves out of a job are only partially correct. Like any tool, empowerment evaluation is designed to address a specific evaluative need. It is not a substitute for other forms of evaluative inquiry or appraisal. We are educating others to manage their own affairs in areas they know (or should know) better than we do. At the same time, we are creating new roles for evaluators to help others help themselves.

■ Objectivity

How objective can a self-evaluation be? Objectivity is a relevant concern. We need not, however, belabor the obvious point that science and specifically evaluation have never been neutral. Anyone who has had to roll up her sleeves and get her hands dirty in program evaluation or policy arenas is aware that evaluation, like any other dimension of life, is political, social, cultural, and economic. It rarely produces a single truth or conclusion.[1]

Greene (1997) explained that "social program evaluators are inevitably on somebody's side and not on somebody else's side. The sides chosen by evaluators are most importantly expressed in whose questions are addressed and, therefore, what criteria are used to make judgments about program quality" (p. 25). She points out how Campbell's work (1971) focuses on *policy makers*, Patton's (1997a) on *on-site program administrators and board members*, Stake's (1995) on *on-site program directors and staff*, and Scriven's (1993) on the *needs of program consumers.* These are not neutral positions; they are, in fact, positions of *de facto* advocacy based on the stakeholder focal point in the evaluation.

Objectivity functions along a continuum: It is not an absolute or dichotomous condition of all or none. Fortunately, such objectivity is not essential to being critical. For example, I support programs designed to help dropouts pursue their education and prepare for a career; however, I am highly critical of program implementation efforts. If the program is operating poorly, it is doing a disservice both to former dropouts and to taxpayers.

There are colleagues who believe in an absolute and clear form of objectivity in the field. For example, according to Stufflebeam (1994), "Objectivist evaluations are based on the theory that moral good is objective and independent of personal or merely human feelings. They are firmly grounded in ethical principles, strictly control bias or prejudice in seeking determinations of merit and worth" (p. 326). This position stands in contrast to much of contemporary evaluation and certainly empowerment evaluation. As Berk and Rossi (1976) explain,

Dominant ideologies . . . affect the definitions of evaluation criteria. . . . [E]val-
uation research may validate a particular view of social problems by emphasizing certain outcomes as opposed to others, . . . [and] evaluation research
methodology contributes to the definition of social problems; virtually all
technical issues have an ideological side. (p. 339)

To assume that evaluation is all in the name of science, or that it is separate
from, above, politics or "mere human feelings"—indeed, that evaluation
is objective—is to deceive oneself and to do an injustice to others.

One needs only to scratch the surface of the "objective" world to see
that values, interpretations, and culture shape it. Whose ethical principles
are evaluators grounded in? Do we all come from the same cultural, reli-
gious, or even academic tradition? Such an ethnocentric assumption or as-
sertion flies in the face of our accumulated knowledge about social systems and evaluation. Similarly, assuming that we can "strictly control bias
or prejudice" is naive, given the wealth of literature available on the subject, ranging from discussions about cultural interpretation to reactivity in
experimental design (see Conrad, 1994; Fetterman, 1982.)

■ Bias

What about participant or program bias? The process of conducting an empowerment evaluation requires the appropriate involvement of stakeholders. The entire group—not a single individual, not the external evaluator or an internal manager—is responsible for conducting the evaluation.
The group thus can serve as a check on individual members, moderating
their various biases and agendas.

No individual operates in a vacuum. Everyone is accountable in one
fashion or another and thus has an interest or agenda to protect. As noted
earlier, a school district may have a 5-year plan designed by the superintendent; a graduate school may have to satisfy requirements of an accreditation association; an outside evaluator may have an important but demanding sponsor pushing either time lines or results, or may be
influenced by training to use one theoretical approach rather than another.

In a sense, empowerment evaluation minimizes the effect of these biases by making them an explicit part of the process. The example of a self-
evaluation in a performance appraisal is useful again here. An employee
negotiates with his or her supervisor about job goals, strategies for accom-

plishing them, documentation of progress, and even the time line. In turn, the employee works with clients to come to an agreement about acceptable goals, strategies, documentation, and time lines. All of this activity takes place within corporate, institutional, and community goals, objectives, and aspirations. The larger context, like theory, provides a lens through which to design a self-evaluation. Self-serving forms of documentation do not easily persuade supervisors and clients. Once an employee loses credibility with a supervisor, it is difficult to regain it. The employee thus has a vested interest in providing authentic and credible documentation. Credible data (as agreed on by supervisor and client in negotiation with the employee) serve both the employee and the supervisor during the performance appraisal process.

Applying this approach to the program or community level, superintendents, accreditation agencies, and other "clients" require credible data. As discussed earlier, participants in an empowerment evaluation thus negotiate goals, strategies, documentation, and time lines. Credible data can be used to advocate for program expansion, redesign, and/or improvement. This process is an open one, placing a check on self-serving reports. It provides an infrastructure and network to combat institutional injustices. Program staff members and participants are typically more critical of their own program than an external evaluator, often because they are more familiar with their program and would like to see it serve its purpose(s) more effectively.[2] Empowerment evaluation is successful because it adapts and responds to existing decision-making and authority structures on their own terms (see Fetterman, 1993b, 1993c, 1994a, 1995). It also provides an opportunity and a forum to challenge authority and managerial façades by providing data about actual program operations—from the ground up. The approach is particularly valuable for disenfranchised people and programs to ensure that their voices are heard and that real problems are addressed.

■ Positions of Privilege

Empowerment evaluation is grounded in my work with the most marginalized and disenfranchised populations, ranging from urban school systems to community health programs in South African townships, who have educated me about what is possible in communities overwhelmed by violence, poverty, disease, and neglect. They have also repeatedly sensitized me to the power of positions of privilege. One dominant group has the vision, makes and changes the rules, enforces the standards, and needs never question its own position or seriously consider any other. In such a view, differences become deficits rather than additive elements of culture. People in positions of privilege dismiss the contributions of a multicultural world. They create rational policies and procedures that systematically deny full participation in their community to people who think and behave differently.

Evaluators cannot afford to be unreflective about the culturally embedded nature of our profession. There are many tacit prejudgments and omissions embedded in our primarily Western thought and behavior. These values, which are often assumed to be superior, are considered by many as natural. Western philosophies, however, have privileged their own traditions and used them to judge others who may not share them, disparaging such factors as ethnicity and gender. In addition, they systematically exclude other ways of knowing.[3] Scriven's (1991, pp. 260–261) discussion about perspectival evaluation is instructive in this context, highlighting the significance of adopting multiple perspectives, including new perspectives.

We need to keep open minds, including alternative ways of knowing— but not empty heads. Skepticism is healthy; cynicism, blindness, and condemnation are not, particularly for emerging evaluative forms and adaptations. New approaches in evaluation and even new ways of knowing are needed if we are to expand our knowledge base and respond to pressing needs. As Campbell (1994) states, we should not "reject the new epistemologies out of hand. . . . Any specific challenge to an unexamined presumption of ours should be taken seriously" (p. 293). Patton (1994) might be right that "the world will not end in a subjective bang, but in a boring whimper as voices of objectivity [drift] off into the chaos" (p. 312).

Evaluation must change and adapt as the environment changes, or it will either be overshadowed by new developments or, as a result of its unresponsiveness and irrelevance, follow the path of the dinosaurs to extinction. People are demanding much more of evaluation and are not tolerant of the limited role of the outside expert who has no knowledge of or vested interest in their program or community. Participation, collaboration, and empowerment are becoming requirements in many community-based evaluations, not recommendations. Program participants are conducting empowerment and other forms of self- or participatory evaluations with or without those of us in the evaluation community. I think it is healthier for all parties concerned to work together to improve practice rather than ignore, dismiss, and condemn evaluation practice; otherwise, we foster the development of separate worlds operating and unfolding in isolation from each other.

■ Conclusion

Empowerment evaluation is designed to be used by program staff members and participants. Rigor can be maintained, particularly with evaluation coaching. However, usefulness supercedes academic precision. In addition, empowerment evaluation fulfills a specific need in the field. It is also designed to influence traditional evaluation, not replace it. Empowerment evaluation views objectivity along a continuum, rather than as an absolute. It provides program staff members and participants with an opportunity to have their voice heard. Bias becomes an asset in the sense that multiple perspectives and opinions are placed on the table in a community context, rather than a single voice or bias dominating decision making. Finally, empowerment evaluation helps lift the blinders that unreflective positions of privilege impose on program staff members, participants, evaluators, and policy decision makers.

This discussion about caveats and concerns sets the stage for an additional critical examination of this approach in Chapter 8 with the larger aim of distinguishing empowerment evaluation from other forms of evaluation. It is facilitated by some of the most prominent members of the evaluation community, specifically Michael Patton and Michael Scriven.

■ Notes

1. There are evaluators who believe neutrality exists, independent of significant cultural and political contextual variables. For example, in the context of a discussion about self-referent evaluation, Stufflebeam (1994) states,

> As a practical example of this, in the coming years U.S. teachers will have the opportunity to have their competence and effectiveness examined against the standards of the National Board for Professional Teaching Standards and if they pass to become nationally certified. (p. 331)

Regardless of one's position on this issue, evaluation in this context is a political act. What Stufflebeam considers an opportunity, some teachers consider a threat to their livelihood, status, and role in the community. This can be a screening device in which social class, race, and ethnicity are significant variables. The goal is "improvement," but the questions of for whom and at what price remain valid. Evaluation in this context or any other is not neutral: It is for one group a force of social change, for another a tool to reinforce the status quo.

2. There are many useful mechanisms to enhance a self-critical mode. Beginning with an overall assessment of the program often leads to inflated ratings. However, asking program participants to assess program components before asking for an overall assessment facilitates the self-critical process. In addition, allowing individuals to comment on successful parts of the program typically enables them to comment openly on problematic components.

3. Some evaluators are convinced that there is only one position and one sacred text in evaluation, justifying exclusion or excommunication for any "violations" or wrong thinking (see Stufflebeam, 1994).

8

A DIALOGUE

Distinguishing Empowerment Evaluation From Other Approaches

> He that wrestles with us strengthens our nerves and
> sharpens our skills. Our antagonist is our helper.
>
> —Edmund Burke

One of the benefits of belonging to a larger community of learners, such as the evaluation community, is that colleagues take the time to enter into an intellectual engagement with the aim of refining and distinguishing innovations and adaptations in the field. Literally hundreds of colleagues have provided valuable contributions to the development of empowerment evaluation. Their discussions have been mined for every ounce of insight to build and refine this approach. This chapter is in large part a product or synthesis of these scholarly contributions. In addition, it is a contribution toward Shadish's (1998) call to "situate empowerment evaluation in a larger context of similar and dissimilar theories" (p. 12).

A discussion in the literature about empowerment evaluation with Michael Patton and Michael Scriven stands out as having been particularly fruitful in helping to distinguish empowerment evaluation from other approaches. Our exchanges have highlighted various issues critical to understanding and using empowerment evaluation, including the following questions:

- How is empowerment evaluation similar to and different from collaborative and participatory approaches?
- Does empowerment evaluation exist along a continuum of greater and lesser degrees of fidelity to the ideal?
- How do you identify the target group in empowerment evaluation?
- What is empowerment evaluation's relationship to stakeholder and utilization-focused evaluation?
- Who has ownership in an empowerment evaluation?
- What is the role of advocacy in empowerment evaluation?
- What are some of the problems associated with political correctness?
- What is the role of accountability?
- Why is the consumer focus important?
- What is the worldwide movement issue?
- What is the role and value of hard work in empowerment evaluation?
- What is the problem with maintaining a distance in empowerment evaluation?
- What is the relationship between internal and external evaluation in empowerment evaluation?
- When is an empowerment evaluator an evaluator, and when is she a consultant?
- What is the value of devolving evaluation responsibility?
- What is the value and significance of process use in empowerment evaluation?

Process use is an excellent point of departure in this regard because of its significance for the utilization of evaluation findings and recommendations.

■ Process Use Focus

Patton (1997a) and Vanderplaat (1995) accurately place empowerment evaluation in the larger context of emancipatory research. In addition,

Patton helps to identify empowerment evaluation's unique contribution to the field by focusing on its explicit commitment to fostering self-determination (p. 148) and building capacity (p. 155). Patton captures a significant part of the theory behind empowerment evaluation in his review of the approach: "A fourth purpose [of empowerment evaluation] . . . is teaching evaluation logic and skills as a way of building capacity for ongoing self-assessment. In modeling terms, such skills are seen as enhancing the capacity for self-determination" (p. 156).

Building on this point, Patton identifies a critical feature of empowerment evaluation: "empowerment evaluation as process use" (p. 156).

The new emphasis on *process use* directs attention to the impacts of participating in an evaluation *in addition* to generating findings, impacts that derive from using the logic, employing the reasoning, and being guided by the values that undergird the evaluation profession (e.g., Fournier, 1995; House, 1980). These impacts include enhanced mutual understanding among those participating in the evaluation, support and reinforcement for the program intervention, program, organizational, and community development (e.g., developmental evaluation, Patton, 1994), and increased participant engagement in and ownership of program and evaluation processes. Participation and collaboration can lead to a long-term commitment to use evaluation logic and techniques thereby building a culture of learning among those involved.

The cases in *Empowerment Evaluation* [Fetterman, Kaftarian, & Wandersman, 1996] document the ways in which participants in an evaluation can come to value both the processes and findings of an evaluation. A theme running through the book is that learning to see the world as an evaluator sees it, often has a lasting impact on those who participate in an evaluation—an impact that can be greater and last longer than the findings that result from that same evaluation, especially where those involved can apply that learning to future planning and evaluation situations. This capacity-building emphasis of empowerment evaluation has helped illuminate the nature and importance of process use for those who study and theorize about utilization of evaluation. (p. 156)

The results of Cousins's (1998) North American survey of evaluators and practitioners also highlight the significance of process use, revealing that "participation caused [practitioners] to rethink their practice and to question basic assumptions about it" (p. 8; for additional discussion about the relationship between the impact of evaluation and the actual process of carrying out the study, see also Ayers, 1987; Cousins, Donohue, & Bloom, 1996; Cousins & Earl, 1992, 1995; Greene, 1988; Patton, 1994, 1997b; Preskill, 1994; Timar, 1994; Torres, Preskill, & Piontek, 1996).

■ Collaborative, Participatory, and Empowerment Evaluation

There is an overlap between collaborative, participatory, and empowerment approaches in practice. Synergistic strength is a function of overlapping, interrelated, and reinforcing characteristics and features. Empowerment evaluation requires collaborative and participatory activities. Collaboration and participation are features that help characterize this approach, along with an explicit commitment to self-determination and capacity building. However, greater conceptual clarity between similar approaches is merited. Collaboration, for example, covers the broadest range of activity, ranging from an evaluator's initial (minimal) consultation with key stakeholder to full-scale collaboration with program staff members and participants in every stage of the evaluation. Participatory approaches range from program staff members and participants participating in a researcher or evaluator's agenda to direct participation in the design and implementation of an evaluation. Typically, however, participatory approaches begin with an evaluator soliciting participation in their effort and attempt to transfer power, until participants dominate the effort. Empowerment evaluation typically begins where many participatory approaches conclude—in the hands of program staff members and participants.

Cousins, Donohue, and Bloom (1996) provide a useful picture of this continuum[1] by contrasting them according to two dimensions: depth of participation and control of evaluation technical decision making. According to their conceptual framework, empowerment evaluation (Fetterman, 1994a, 1995; Fetterman, Kaftarian, & Wandersman, 1996) is at the furthest end of the continuum in terms of extensive participation and stakeholder controlled. Participatory evaluation (Brunner & Guzman, 1989) is second along the continuum with the same degree of extensive participation, but in the next category of balanced control. Stakeholder-based evaluation (Bryk, 1983) was classified as moderate participation and evaluator controlled. These approaches were contrasted with objectivist evaluation (Stufflebeam, 1994), an approach that does not fall within any of the col-

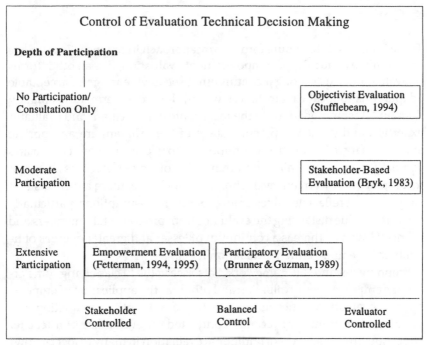

Figure 8.1. Collaborative Evaluation Process Dimensions. Based on a figure in "Collaborative evaluation in North America: Evaluators' self-reported opinions, practices and consequences," by J. B. Cousins, J. J. Donohue, and G. A. Bloom, 1996, *Evaluation Practice, 17*(3), p. 211.

laborative, participatory, or empowerment evaluation models. It was classified as noncollaborative, and categorized as *no participation/consultation only* and *evaluator controlled.* (See Figure 8.1 for a graphic representation of these categories; see Weiss, 1998, for an equally valid comparison of three stages along a continuum of evaluator roles—i.e., empowerment evaluation, collaborative evaluation, and stakeholder evaluation; see also King, 1998, and Whitmore, 1998, for additional discussion about participatory evaluation.)

These initial efforts at distinguishing between similar approaches should not be used to divide and weaken strong bonds and relationships. There is more in common than different between collaborative, participatory, and empowerment evaluation approaches.

■ Continuum

There is no absolute or pure form of any approach in practice. Evaluations approximate an ideal type. Empowerment evaluation, like all other forms of evaluation, exists along a continuum. I see a wide range of acceptable adaptations to local circumstances within the empowerment evaluation domain.[2] Accommodations to the local context, participant and evaluator expertise, and the developmental stage of the program are appropriate and necessary to be effective. It is important to take into account intent and context when determining the boundaries of any effort. This does not mean that empowerment evaluation is all-inclusive; there are efforts that simply do not reflect its values or incorporate its assumptions, particularly those that value distancing the evaluator from program staff members and clients. However, there is a continuum of lesser and greater degrees of fidelity to an empowerment evaluation ideal.

Stepping beyond this framework, I also see value in classifying some efforts as empowerment evaluation and others as the application of empowerment evaluation concepts and techniques to other evaluation approaches. For example, I recently conducted an evaluation of a teacher education program.[3] It was a traditional evaluation in many respects; however, I applied empowerment evaluation concepts and techniques to this effort, including asking student focus groups (consumers) to identify and rate the most significant features of the program. This is an example of applying relevant empowerment evaluation concepts and techniques without conducting a pure or full-blown empowerment evaluation.

■ Target Population

Empowerment evaluation efforts have been focused on traditionally disenfranchised, oppressed, and economically impoverished populations.[4] However, disenfranchised and oppressed people also exist in traditional academic, government, and business organizations as well as in ghettos and undeveloped areas. In addition, the approach is rooted in work with individuals with disabilities. Self-determination is potentially applicable to human beings on every level of the social and economic scale. Gene Glass (personal communication, 1998) has insightfully observed that empowerment is both a psychological and political force. Psychologically, everyone can benefit from being more self-determined. Politically, there are limits.

■ Criteria and Similarities With Stakeholder and Utilization-Focused Evaluation

Empowerment evaluation is strongly influenced by stakeholder and utilization-focused evaluations, as Patton (1997a, p. 148) has observed. These similarities are not coincidental. Empowerment evaluation should resemble them in many respects. In fact it may be considered a necessary but not sufficient characteristic of this approach (see also Greene, 1988, for an extensive discussion about stakeholder participation and utilization in evaluation).

■ Ownership

Evaluation ownership and group advocacy (discussed in greater detail in the next section) are compatible and reinforcing, but not harmonious. Ownership is not a simple step. It requires hard work on behalf of the group and the empowerment evaluator. In essence, the locus of power rests primarily with the group engaged in its self-evaluation (as guided by a critical friend in the profession). Even groups who request an empowerment evaluation may not fully understand the open democratic nature of the experience. Many have been socialized within another framework and easily retreat into the relative safety or ease of well-defined boundaries and expectations, including opting to hand over the evaluation to the "professional evaluator" (a typical stage in empowerment evaluation that should initially be resisted to foster self-reliance and avoid dependency). It is a routine struggle. The key, however, is ownership. The group—the program staff members and the participants—need to generate ideas concerning how best to collect the data and analyze it. From this effort, participants learn to use documents they are already collecting (but in a more focused and systematic fashion) and to make the evaluation process part of their daily lives, including regular meetings. As groups begin to own the evaluation as a tool for self-determination and program improvement, responsible advocacy becomes a natural next step. The findings lend themselves to that kind of use. Advocacy is appropriate when and if the evaluation findings merit it.

■ Advocacy

The issues of advocacy and accountability were briefly discussed above and in Chapter 1, in which advocacy was explored in terms of a facet of empowerment evaluation. In this chapter, advocacy is used to help highlight similarities and differences between empowerment evaluation and other approaches. For example, Greene's (1997) explicit value commitment to democratic pluralism in evaluation is shared by empowerment evaluators, viewing "evaluation as a force for democratizing public conversation about important public issues" (p. 29). However, she separated this position from a particular stance toward a particular program.

A thornier issue for some evaluators, which this discussion raises, is the role of the coach or evaluator assisting a group as an advocate. Empowerment evaluators first and foremost assist others, including helping them to evaluate their program and gather data that they may then use to advocate for changes warranted by the data. Following the same guidelines used by action ethnographers, empowerment evaluators remove themselves from playing a power role. The insiders or participants design and implement the evaluation, with the evaluator's guidance and assistance. The decision to implement a specific innovation, or to advocate for additional resources, remains in the hands of staff members and participants. They control the means of making their own changes. However, this approach (removing oneself as much as possible from a power role) can only take place in a community that has the potential to determine its own fate. Empowerment evaluation can help a group become more cohesive or empowered to do something about its plight. However, this approach requires that the group have the capacity to develop a binding decision-making process. It also requires that the group control the resources necessary to make the changes it desires.

Similar to action anthropologists (Tax, 1958) who advocate for the people they work with, empowerment evaluators can serve in the same capacity (again, if the findings merit such advocacy). The empowerment evaluator coach may shift into a new role as a program or group advocate, after participants have evaluated their program or social condition and proposed ideal solutions to their problems. However, program staff members and participants typically advocate for themselves. It can be disempowering for the empowerment evaluator to advocate for a group that is capable of speaking for itself.

An advocacy role is not new in evaluation. An essential part of any evaluation is the communication of evaluation findings to the sponsors and to the public. Evaluation findings do not speak for themselves; they are carefully orchestrated and choreographed events. The evaluator thus can, and typically does, serve as an advocate during the presentation of traditional evaluation findings.

After conducting an evaluation of a national program for dropouts, our evaluation team prepared a Joint Dissemination Review Panel Submission to improve the program's credibility and its chances of securing future funding. Empowerment evaluators may write in public forums to change public opinion and provide relevant information about a situation at opportune moments in the policy decision-making forum. The presentation of evaluation findings to a concerned public is the evaluator's legitimate responsibility. The presentation of evaluation findings here aims to influence the use of the information. In empowerment evaluation, as in traditional evaluation, advocacy is legitimate and ethical, but should take place after sufficient and appropriate evaluation activity has been completed. Moreover, program staff members, participants, and funders should take the lead in this specific program advocacy activity.

House and Howe's (House, 1998; House & Howe, in press) views about deliberative democracy and social justice shed light on how advocacy is understood and practiced in empowerment evaluation:

> Advocacy in the misdirected sense would mean that one enters the study already convinced that the African Americans are right and the service providers wrong, or vice versa, regardless of the facts. This is not the proper role for evaluators.
>
> Our notion of the public interest in evaluation is one of deliberative democracy in which the evaluation informs public opinion objectively by including views and interests, promoting dialogue, and fostering deliberation directed towards reaching valid conclusions. Objectivity is supplied by inclusion, dialogue, and deliberation and by the evaluation expertise the professional evaluator brings to bear. Evaluators cannot escape being committed to some notion of democracy and the public interest. The question is how explicit and defensible it is." (House, 1998, p. 236)

■ Political Correctness

Political correctness in any evaluation, including empowerment evaluation merits attention. It can operate in the background like a subtle but pervasive noise creeping into one's consciousness. I, like Patton (1997a), have found that even groups heavily influenced by politically correct rhetoric generally take ownership and responsibility for their members' actions. However, I am concerned about the potential tyranny of radical groups, left or right. The question is, who is allowed to make meaning? There are individuals who successfully hijack and commandeer an agenda with a seemingly endless string of well-timed questions about process, interrupting others and thus minimizing their ability to contribute. These individuals are less interested in facilitating social change or justice than in controlling others. Questions (even long-winded ones) about process and decision making are appropriate; however, such individuals can exploit these conventions for very different, controlling motives. Less conscious acts by well-intentioned members of a group include body language, tone, and facial expressions that demean others and thus shut them out of the dialogue. Politically correct "police" ready to sanction rather than educate and to narrow the norms of acceptable behavior are disempowering as well as controlling, and thus can undermine any evaluation effort.

■ Accountability

Accountability is an important feature of empowerment evaluation. Patton (1997a) accurately captures the philosophical foundation of empowerment evaluation when he comments, "The philosophy comes down to this: the highest form of accountability is self-accountability" (p. 161). It does not end there, however. As I discussed in Chapter 5, concerning the accreditation self-study in higher education empowerment evaluation, the group decided to close one of its programs and merge a second program. Cutting and consolidating one's own programs represents one of the highest levels of accountability—internally or externally. Although empowerment evaluation has a contribution to make in traditional areas normally associated with external accountability, its focus is on development and self-accountability.

■ Consumer Focus

Empowerment evaluation has a consumer focus. Scriven (1997a, 1997b) is frequently associated with emphasizing the consumer's role in evaluation. This is a useful reminder and contribution to combat the self-serving complacency that can result in a lessened role for the consumer. There is a natural tendency to focus on those who have the funds to pay for an evaluation or those who are the easiest to access. The consumer's voice is often excluded from the evaluation table.

At the same time, not all evaluations (including empowerment evaluations) need to be exclusively consumer focused. Consumers are only one part of the puzzle, and staff members' and managers' concerns and constraints need to be taken into consideration as well, if we aspire to capture a complete picture of the situation and if recommendations are to be used or implemented. Moreover, there is nothing wrong with beginning to develop a critical mass of program staff members when attempting to build and cultivate an evaluative community of learners, because they are initially a more cohesive entity. Furthermore, the contrast between program staff members and participants or consumers is not entirely valid on the face of it, as program staff members as well as participants need to become more self-determined and help others. There are real differences between staff members and consumer interests in theory; however, the lines between the two in disenfranchised communities are often very fine.

■ Movement

Some colleagues have viewed empowerment evaluation, sometimes fearfully, as a worldwide "movement."[5] This is an understandable reaction, given the pace and scope of adoption by government, foundations, and academe. I understand that this characterization does pay indirect tribute to the widespread interest in this new evaluation approach. However, empowerment evaluation remains simply one of many useful evaluation approaches in use throughout the world. The commitment and enthusiasm associated with this new approach is a function of both the level of engagement required to conduct this kind of effort and the rich, rewarding environment it creates. It is a constructive force designed to help people help themselves using evaluation as a tool, and it establishes a dynamic, evaluative community of learners.

Recent surveys of evaluators and practitioners provide some insight into the changing landscape of evaluation, making it more receptive to collaborative, participatory, and empowerment evaluation approaches. For example, Cousins (1998) reports how practitioners find this kind of evaluative experience rewarding and enjoyable. In addition, Cousins, Donohue, and

Bloom (1996) report how evaluators familiar with this type of approach think that "evaluation can result in fundamental changes in practice"; that it "stimulate[s] practitioners to question fundamental beliefs and assumptions about practice"; that it "help[s] practitioners improve practice"; that it "should educate practitioners about the power and value of evaluation as a planned change strategy"; that it "should help train practitioners to do evaluations"; that "practitioners' participation in evaluation enhances the utilization of evaluation data"; and that "practitioners' participation in evaluation makes the research more responsive to local needs" (p. 216). Preskill and Caracelli (1997) report the following findings from their survey:

> The greatest change from ten years ago, however, is in the importance placed on organizational learning, participatory, and practitioner-centered action research or empowerment approaches to evaluation. Respondents believe that evaluation can not only facilitate organizational learning, but that evaluation can be a powerful change strategy. (p. 221)

In addition, they reported that "nearly all of the respondents (95%) agree that evaluators should take responsibility for involving stakeholders in the evaluation process" (p. 221). These findings convey a measure of the excitement, commitment, and power associated with this kind of approach.

Empowerment evaluation has gained, over the past several years, a solid presence in professional associations as well. The American Evaluation Association has a Collaborative, Participatory, and Empowerment Evaluation topical interest group with its own Internet home page (<http://www.stanford.edu/~davidf/empowermentevaluation.html>), newsletter, and e-mail listserv. Empowerment evaluations have been well represented in evaluation, education, health, and anthropological association meetings.

Although I do not consider it a movement in the sense Scriven (1997a) or Sechrest (1997) suggests, I do recognize the dedication and commitment of those colleagues conducting quality work in this area, and the intellectual excitement we share in pursuing this path together. This approach is not a complete product of an individual expression or conception; it is an ongoing collective effort to refine and further develop a form of self-evaluation in which traditional evaluation concepts and techniques are used to foster self-determination and program improvement, building capacity in the process.

■ Hard Work

A common question that arises in discussions about empowerment evaluation is whether or not it is more work. Or, as many say, "It sounds like hard work." The answer is yes, but it depends on how you define work. Adopting an empowerment evaluation posture is much harder than telling someone what to do or what the merit or worth of their endeavor is. An evaluation moves along much more quickly and without as much effort when program staff members and participants are not involved in the process on a routine basis. An evaluation is simpler and requires much less work when it reflects a narrower spectrum of the community's interests and concerns, such as the manager's single viewpoint. Building capacity and facilitating empowerment is hard work. However, it is fundamentally an investment in people and the sustainability of their efforts.

Commitment redefines work. As anthropologist Ruth Benedict has said, "The happiest excitement in life is to be convinced that one is fighting for all one is worth on behalf of some clearly seen and deeply felt good." A commitment to what one believes in can turn drudgery and "hard work" into a labor of love. As an evaluative folk culture is developed in a group or organization, the effort begins to flow. Mihaly Csikszentmihalyi described this phenomenon in his book *Creativity: Flow and the psychology of discovery and invention* (1990). He presents there a number of case examples in which time appears to pass more quickly when an individual engages in this psychological state. Empowerment evaluation works in precisely the same way, once an evaluative folk culture is established and maintained. People are energized instead of drained. There is a real sense of accomplishment in empowerment evaluation experiences. As one participant in an evaluation said, "I remember when we were at our busiest period and everyone was overwhelmed but no one complained. You just really got into it." Although efforts are made in empowerment evaluation to minimize additional work for program staff members and participants, there should be no illusion or misconception. Empowerment evaluation requires hard work—the kind of work that has the potential to capture the imagination, feed the soul, and free the spirit.

■ Distance

Distance is valued as a form of independence and objectivity for some evaluators.[6] According to Scriven (1997b),

> There are many ways to do distanced evaluations, but it is perhaps worth mentioning that in goal-free evaluation, which works very well in many circumstances, the evaluator not only never talks to program staff at all, but never reads the program rationale documents. (pp. 484–485)

I have conducted portions of audits without interviewing program personnel and relying on extant data alone. It is revealing how informative this approach can be; however, it is the least efficient way to understand a typical situation, let alone determine a program's merit or worth. It may be required in certain efforts, such as in investigative evaluations and audits, when it would be inappropriate to "tip your hand." However, to function in this capacity in the majority of collaborative or empowerment evaluations is inappropriate and inauthentic.

People represent one of the most significant links to valid and reliable findings. I believe the best data are secured through close observation of people and interaction with them, not through distancing oneself from them. Moreover, distancing oneself loses a complex web of interactions and considerations. Talking with them and spending time immersed in their daily lives captures the richness of people's lives and what they bring to a program on all levels (see Fetterman 1989, 1998c).

■ Internal and External Evaluation

Empowerment evaluation and external evaluation are not mutually exclusive. Empowerment evaluation involves the institutionalization of evaluation, making it part of the routine planning and management of a program. It also uses the determination of worth and value to facilitate illumination and liberation.

Many funders and accrediting agencies have found self-evaluations to be of much greater value to staff members than external evaluations—particularly for the purpose of capacity building. In addition, the institutional integrity and the power of internal evaluations and audits directed toward finding problems and bring them to the attention of management can have far-reaching effects on the direction and operations of large organizations, as long as the evaluators have the ear of management and report to the highest level of authority.

Scriven (1997a) and I (Fetterman, 1996a) agree on this point:

> One should not have to add that external evaluators will sometimes miss deep problems that are obvious to Staff and that they often have less credibility with Staff than the empowerment evaluator, and often for that or other reasons, there is less chance that their recommendations will be implemented. The dilemma of whether to use external or internal evaluation is as false as that between quantitative and qualitative methods. The solution is always to use the best of both, not just one or the other. (Scriven, 1997a, p. 12)

Clearly, as discussed earlier, a second set of (external) eyes often helps the group avoid blind spots and provides another vantage point outside the internal vision of the program. Complementing an external evaluation's contributions, empowerment evaluation provides an extraordinarily rich source of information for external assessments. Empowerment evaluation and external evaluation thus can be mutually reinforcing efforts.

Scriven (1997a) envisions a bond or combination of empowerment evaluation and traditional external evaluation in the future:

> Making empowerment evaluation a clearly defined part of good evaluation, where appropriate (which is often), and with strong controls on bias (e.g., by using consumer representatives and an external evaluator), is a relatively new emphasis which could be highly valuable. If combined with serious (third-party) evaluation of the results of doing this, it could represent a major contribution to the evaluation repertoire. In my judgment, the best future for empowerment evaluation lies in this direction. (p. 174)

I agree that this is one trajectory into the future. However, I also see empowerment evaluation standing alone when the purpose of the evaluation is in the development domain.

■ Empowerment Evaluator or Consultant

The norm in empowerment evaluation is an immersed coach or facilitator, engaged in routine aspects of the self-evaluation. *Empowerment evaluators* participate in the evaluation effort with program staff members and participants. Training in empowerment evaluations is coterminous with the evaluation design and implementation, and thus is evaluation. It is similar to conducting evaluations with students or junior colleagues; we are teaching them while we are conducting the evaluation. As many apprentices know, this is one of the best ways to learn a trade. Teaching hospitals are examples of environments that depend on this blending of teaching and practice.

However, coaches or facilitators may serve as empowerment evaluation consultants, rather than empowerment evaluation evaluators. *Empowerment evaluation consultants* advise about ongoing empowerment evaluations. When I serve on an advisory board and provide advice about a college's ongoing empowerment evaluation, but am not directly involved in the daily affairs of the evaluation, I am serving as a consultant in an empowerment evaluation. Similarly, when training or teaching people how to conduct their own evaluations separately from the actual evaluation at hand, the evaluator is serving in a useful consulting capacity. (For additional discussion about the distinction, see Scriven, 1997a, p. 172.)

■ Devolving Responsibility

Scriven (1997a) and I agree that "devolving some of the responsibility for evaluation is good. A program whose staff are not doing reasonably good evaluation of their own program is incompetently staffed, at some or all levels. Empowerment evaluation is doing something important to reduce that deficit" (Scriven, 1997a, p. 174).

■ Watershed Moments

There are watershed moments, issues, and conceptualizations that help move intellectual discourse along to the next step. My own debate with Stufflebeam (Stufflebeam, 1994; Fetterman, 1995) represents one moment in the dialogue: differing stands useful in clarifying opposing relationships. Discussions with Patton, Scriven, and Sechrest (Fetterman, 1997a, 1997b; Patton, 1997a; Scriven, 1997a; Sechrest, 1997) in the literature represented significant advances in thinking about empowerment evaluation. However, I think Chelimsky and Shadish's *Evaluation for the 21st Cen-*

tury: A Handbook (1997) represented a watershed moment in this evaluative discussion, allowing us to break free from the artificial barriers we created. Rather than argue about whether or not empowerment evaluation fits into evaluation, Chelimsky (1997) provided a useful framework for our discussion using three different evaluation purposes:

1. Accountability (e.g., to measure results or efficiency)

2. Development (e.g., to strengthen institutions)

3. Knowledge (e.g., to acquire a more profound understanding in some specific area or field)

Chelimsky's description of the second of these purposes is most pertinent to the present discussion. As Chelimsky explains,

> for other purposes . . . —such as strengthening institutions, improving agency performance, or helping managers think through their planning, evaluation, and reporting tasks—evaluators are faced with a different type of question, in particular, whether others can be assisted to develop a culture of evaluation that will build capacity for better performance. This kind of question calls for formative types of evaluation using developmental methods, such as the participatory analyses described by Fetterman (see Chapter 27 [Chelimsky & Shadish, 1997]). These methods usually have the goal of empowering agency people rather than determining the results of agency programs, but the latter may also be a part of the developmental focus. In such a case (see Wholey, Chapter 8, and Mawhood, Chapter 9 [Chelimsky & Shadish, 1997]), independent evaluators employing different methods can be (and have been) asked to validate the findings established by these internal collaborations of evaluators and agency (or program) actors. (pp. 9–10)

This conceptual framework was not designed to be exhaustive or mutually exclusive but it did allow us to entertain a more fruitful exchange. Instead of talking past each other or arguing about a primarily developmental approach from an exclusively accountability perspective, criteria appropriate to each purpose was discussed in a rational and precise manner. Empowerment evaluation's greatest strength is clearly in the developmental purpose domain, with contributions to be made in the accountability and knowledge purposes of evaluation.

■ Conclusion

Colleagues from around the globe have contributed to our exploration and understanding of empowerment evaluation. Two prominent colleagues have been singled out for their contributions to this new approach, as part of the larger scholarly community. The agreements, challenges, and questions help refine empowerment evaluation, helping to firmly establish its place in the field. As I stated in my 1993 presidential address to the American Evaluation Association, "the ultimate test of any new approach is that as it becomes more clearly defined, useful, and acceptable, it becomes absorbed into the mainstream of evaluation. I look forward to the day when it will be simply one more tool in the evaluator's toolbox" (1994a, p. 12). Empowerment evaluation has become a powerful tool for many evaluators; transcending my own vision. The next chapter explores the Internet's role in helping so many evaluators add this tool to their toolbox.

■ Notes

1. Cousins, Donohue, and Bloom's (1996) framework views collaboration as the overarching concept or approach with empowerment and participatory forms subsumed within that classification. However, other evaluators view collaboration as its own distinct category, separate from participatory and empowerment approaches.

2. Whereas Patton (1997a) places empowerment evaluation strictly within the bounds of liberation, I take a more inclusive view (Fetterman, 1997a).

3. A copy of the evaluation report to the president of Stanford University on the teacher preparation program can be downloaded in PDF format from the following site: <http://www.stanford.edu/~davidf/step.html>.

4. Patton (1997a) is correct in identifying the disenfranchised as the primary target population for empowerment evaluation. However, once again I adopt a much wider vision of appropriate applications and populations.

5. Scriven (1997a) explains "What began as a book review has thus been somewhat enlarged in scope to become a review and critique of a movement that is now an important part of the evaluation scene" (p. 1). Sechrest (1997) also characterized empowerment evaluation as a movement, and thus this characterization merits additional comment.

6. As Scriven (1997b) points out,

the preceding remarks are not just about summative evaluation, but also about formative evaluation. . . . Formative evaluation is, to a large extent, best designed as summative evaluation of an early version, with particular attention to components or dimensions rather than a holistic account (because this facilitates improvement), and provided directly to the program director or staff rather than to external decision makers. It should be contrasted with a midcourse summative evaluation, on which continuance is often dependent. The latter can be holistic and is reported to an external client, who may or may not reveal it to the evaluees. For both, a high degree of distancing is desirable. (pp. 498–499).

THE WORLD WIDE WEB

Using the Internet as a Tool to Disseminate Empowerment Evaluation Worldwide

The new electronic interdependence recreates the world in the image of a small village.

—*Marshall McLuhan*

Empowerment evaluation has become a worldwide phenomenon since its introduction in 1993 at the American Evaluation Association (Fetterman, 1994a). It has required hard work and a series of successful efforts. Empowerment evaluation's acceptance has also been in part a function of timing. Evaluators were already using forms of participatory self-assessment or were prepared to use it because it represented the next logical step in evaluation practice for them and their clients. Funders and clients were focusing on program improvement and capacity building. A critical match between people and common interests was made with an underlying and often implicit commitment to fostering self-determination.

The widespread use of this evaluation approach, however, was also a result of its appearance on the Internet. The Internet's ability to disseminate information quickly on a global scale provided an invaluable communication tool for empowerment evaluation. The Internet and related communication technologies (i.e., e-mail, listservs, on-line surveys, videoconferencing, virtual classrooms, and communication centers) not only aided the dissemination of ideas regarding empowerment evaluation, but resulting on-line discussions also led to refinements of the evaluation process itself. This book about empowerment evaluation was first placed online in a virtual conference, and revisions were made based on on-line feedback. Similarly, on-line empowerment evaluation surveys generated almost immediate feedback, quantifying various empowerment evaluator characteristics, such as age, gender, socioeconomic status, and political orientation, as well as a recommended list of useful tools in the field. Communication technologies have also been used to facilitate discussions among evaluation participants and empowerment evaluation coaches by allowing ongoing asynchronous and synchronous discussions without accompanying time investments required by face-to-face meetings. This rapid distribution and acceptance of new ideas offers a model for colleagues in any field.

Brief discussions in earlier chapters about the background, theory, steps, case examples, standards, caveats, and distinguishing characteristics of empowerment evaluation provided a powerful insight into the approach. This chapter, however, focuses on the synergistic link between the approach and the Internet as a powerful dissemination tool. The Internet has been an invaluable dissemination model in this regard.

■ Internet and Related Technologies: An Effective Dissemination Model

Internet

The Internet has greatly facilitated the distribution of knowledge about and the use of empowerment evaluation. Home pages, listservs, virtual classrooms and conferences, on-line surveys, videoconferencing on the Internet, and publishing on the Internet represent powerful tools that allow one to communicate with large numbers of people, respond to inquiries in a timely fashion, disseminate knowledge, reach isolated populations around the globe, and create a global community of learners. This brief discussion highlights the value of the Internet to facilitate communication about and understanding of empowerment evaluation. All of the web locations discussed in this chapter can be found at <http://www.stanford.edu/~davidf/webresources.html> and <http://www.stanford.edu/~davidf/empowermentevaluation.html>.

Home Pages

The Collaborative, Participatory, and Empowerment Evaluation home page has been a useful mechanism with which to share information about specific projects, professional association activity, book reviews, and related literature. In the spirit of self-reflection and critique, positive and negative reviews of empowerment evaluation are posted on the page (see Altman, 1997; Brown, 1997; Patton, 1997a; Scriven, 1997a; Sechrest, 1997; Wild, 1997). The Collaborative, Participatory, and Empowerment Evaluation topical interest group's electronic newsletter is also accessible through this home page. The home page has been a useful networking tool as well, providing names, e-mail and mailing addresses, and telephone and fax numbers. It provides links to related participatory evaluation sites, such as the *Harvard Evaluation Exchange* and the Health Promotion Internet Lounge's Measurement of Community Empowerment site, free software, InnoNet's Web Evaluation Toolbox (a web-based self-evaluation program), and other web-based evaluation tools to help colleagues conduct their own evaluations (see <http://www.stanford.edu/~davidf/empowermentevaluation.html>).

Listservs

Listservs are lists of e-mail addresses for subscribers with a common interest. Members of the listserv who send messages to the listserv's e-mail address communicate with every listserv subscriber within nanoseconds. Listservs thus provide a simple way to communicate with a large number of people rapidly and inexpensively. The empowerment evaluation listserv also periodically posts employment opportunities and is used to discuss various issues, such as the difference between collaborative, participatory, and empowerment evaluation. Both seasoned colleagues and doctoral students have posted problems or questions and received prompt and generous advice and support.

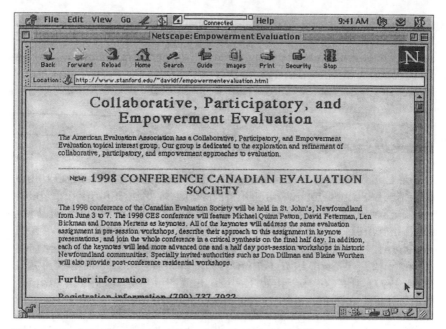

Figure 9.1. A computer screen snapshot of the American Evaluation Association's Collaborative, Participatory, and Empowerment Evaluation home page, highlighting the Canadian Evaluation Society's conference.

Listservs do have some limitations; they can periodically inundate users with marginally relevant discussions. In addition, a misconfigured server can generate an endless loop of postings, burying users with duplicate messages and potentially bringing down an entire computer system. This is a rare occurrence, but one that did bring down an earlier empowerment evaluation listserv, which had to be replaced. Another problem is that information is hard to track and follow after the immediate discussion, because it is not organized or stored according to topic.

Virtual Classrooms and Conference Centers

Virtual classrooms and conference centers allow members to post messages in topical folders in contrast with a listserv's stream of e-mails, which are typically comingled with other unrelated e-mail messages. Folders are labeled by topic, attracting colleagues with similar interests, concerns, and questions to the same location on the web. The benefit of a virtual classroom or conference center over a listserv is that it provides the reader with a thread of conversation; although comments are posted asynchronously, the postings or material read like a conversation. Colleagues have time to think before responding, consult a colleague or a journal, compose their thoughts, and then post a response to an inquiry. In addition, virtual classrooms and conference centers, similar to listservs, enable evaluators to communicate according to their own schedules and in dispersed settings (see Fetterman 1996b for additional detail).

The virtual classroom or conference center has also been an ideal medium in which to work with program participants in remote areas. For example, a group of eighth-grade teachers initially sent an e-mail requesting assistance to conduct an empowerment evaluation of their program in Washington State. It was not possible for my team to travel at the time or to extract us from our daily obligations. Instead, we used the virtual classroom and conference center to interact with the teachers.

The teachers posted their mission and listed critical activities associated with their eighth-grade program in the virtual classroom or conference center. My colleagues and I then commented on their postings, and coached them as they moved from step to step. The virtual classroom and conference center also has a virtual chat section allowing spontaneous and synchronous communication. This feature more closely approximates typical face-to-face interaction because it is "conversation or chatting" (by typing messages back and forth) in real time. However, real-time exchanges limit the users' flexibility in responding, because they have to be sitting at the computers at the same time as their colleagues to communicate. The advantage of asynchronous communication, such as e-mail and the virtual classroom, is that participants do not have to be communicating at the same time; instead they can respond to each other according to their own schedules and time zones (see <http://www.stanford.edu/~davidf/virtual.html> for a virtual classroom demonstration).

On-Line Surveys

On-line or web-based surveys are excellent tools for gathering relevant data about members and take the pulse of a group in an extremely short period of time. The American Evaluation Association's Collaborative, Participatory, and Empowerment Evaluation group used an on-line survey, managed and operated by Flashbase (<http://www.flashbase.com>), an

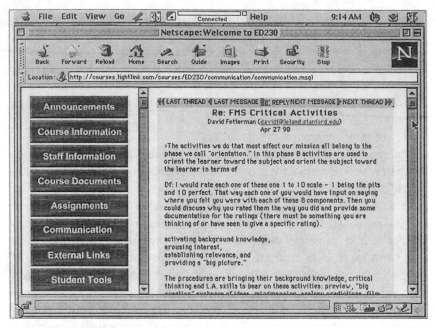

Figure 9.2. A computer screen snapshot of eighth-grade teachers from the state of Washington posting some of their activities in the virtual classroom, along with our critique from Stanford University, Stanford, California.

Internet company, to generate a membership data base and provide an insight into member views about evaluation. The on-line survey is free, and provides user-friendly, modifiable templates to facilitate the process of creating a survey tailored to the group's interests and concerns. The on-line tool automatically sorts the survey data, and creates bar graphs to visually represent the survey results. For example, the first section of the on-line empowerment evaluation survey requested simple demographic data, such as name, address, telephone number, fax number, e-mail address, and web page information. A preexisting form was modified to create this part of the survey. The information derived from this on-line source can be sorted and searched by members at any time, day or night, facilitating contact and communication.

The next section of the survey solicited empowerment evaluator views about the field and themselves. Survey topics and questions included such items as the following:

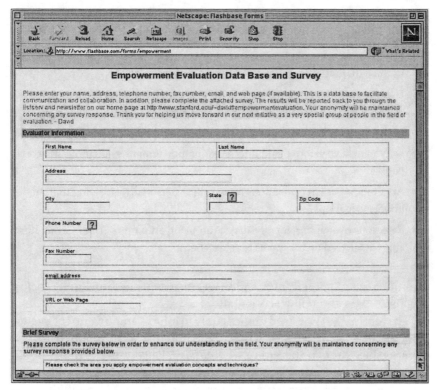

Figure 9.3. This screen snapshot is the first page of the Empowerment Evaluation Survey Form (<http://www.flashbase.com/forms/empowerment>). This section of the survey was used to collect basic demographic data about membership.

- Select the area you apply empowerment evaluation: K–12 education, higher education, health, business, nonprofits, other.
- Where did you hear about empowerment evaluation?
- How often have you facilitated an empowerment evaluation?
- Do you conduct both empowerment evaluations and traditional external evaluations?
- What type of help are you looking for to improve your performance as an empowerment evaluator?
- What is the most common tool you use to facilitate an empowerment evaluation?

- List the best reference you would recommend to a friend to learn more about empowerment evaluation.
- List the most valuable URL or web site you would like to share with our colleagues (to help them conduct an empowerment evaluation).
- Do empowerment evaluations take longer than traditional evaluations?
- Are empowerment evaluations more effective or less effective at building capacity than traditional evaluations?
- Do you believe external and internal or empowerment evaluations are compatible?
- Are empowerment evaluations more or less personally satisfying than traditional evaluations?
- Rate your overall or general satisfaction using an empowerment evaluation approach based on a 1 (poor) to 5 (excellent) scale.

Additional demographic information was also requested, including socioeconomic class and political orientation.

This information was used immediately to inform empowerment evaluators about current practice. The survey findings were reported to the membership through the group's homepage, listserv, and various other forms of communication. The survey results were effectively used to help empowerment evaluators reflect on their own practice, views, affiliations, and characteristics, and report these insights to the larger evaluation community.

In addition to facilitating communication among empowerment evaluators, evaluation colleagues, program staff members, and program participants are already using this on-line tool to facilitate their own empowerment evaluations.

Videoconferencing

Videoconferencing on the Internet involves two or more people seeing and talking to each other through their computer screens or small group conferences in which people converse at Internet reflector sites (places on the Internet where people congregate and talk to each other). The software is free or inexpensive, and there are presently no long-distance charges over the Internet. Videoconferencing software, such as *CU-SeeMe* or *iVisit*, enables people in remote settings to speak to each other audibly or by typing instantaneous messages and to see each other with some mi-

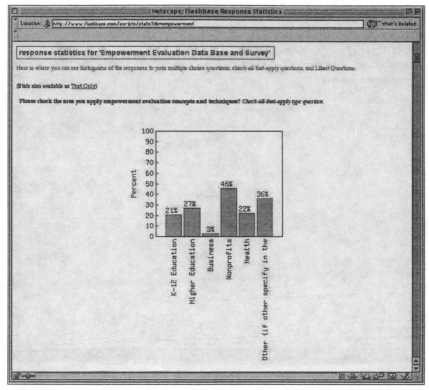

Figure 9.4. This figure was generated by the survey program. It provides an insight into the fields and/or domains in which empowerment evaluators apply this approach.

nor delays (for more information about this tool, see <http://www.stanford.edu/~davidf/videoconference.html>; see also Fetterman, 1996c, 1998e).

Publishing

Internet publishing represents an alternative to printed publications. Some estimates put the number of on-line scholarly journals at over 500 (see <http://ejournals.cic.net>). Refereed on-line journals, such as *Education Policy Analysis Archives* (<http://olam.ed.asu.edu/epaa/>), represent an emerging and exciting vehicle for sharing educational research and evaluation insights and findings in real time. Articles can be reviewed by a larger number of colleagues in a much shorter period of time using e-mail.

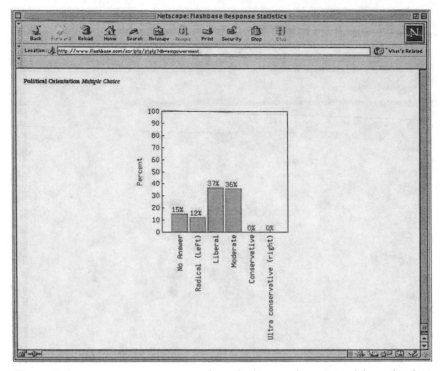

Figure 9.5. A computer screen snapshot of a bar graph generated from the data collected and sorted by the survey program. It presents an important insight into the political orientation of empowerment evaluators, which may influence practice.

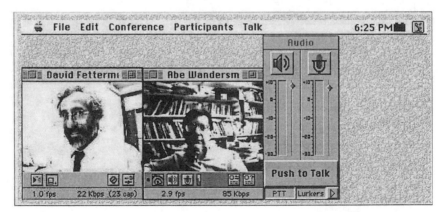

Figure 9.6. A computer screen snapshot of David Fetterman, from Stanford University, and Abraham Wandersman, from the University of South Carolina, videoconferencing about plans for the next empowerment evaluation collection.

In addition, articles can be published electronically much more quickly than in traditional media. Colleagues can critique these electronically published pieces more rapidly, which allows authors to revise their work in less time than it would take to publish an original document traditionally. Moreover, the cost of electronic publication allows journals to be accessed without cost to readers. This medium also allows authors to publish their raw data, including their interviews, linked to the same web page, which allows the reader to analyze the data immediately to sort those data according to their own theoretical orientation. (See an illustration at <http://olam.ed.asu.edu/epaa/v5n1.html>.)

Some colleagues and publishers are concerned about copyright issues. However, norms are developing in this area, and publishing conventions are being successfully applied to this medium (see Burbules & Bruce 1995). I have published articles on the Internet, and our book *Empowerment evaluation: Knowledge and tools for self-assessment and accountability* (Fetterman, Kaftarian, & Wandersman, 1996) was distributed both in traditional print format and over the Internet. We have not experienced any abuse of privilege in this area. We have, however, experienced a rapid and exponentially expanded distribution of ideas. A few examples of Internet publishing are listed below to illustrate how accessible the information is on the Internet: see Fetterman (1998b) concerning empowerment evaluation and the Internet in *Current Issues in Education* at <http://cie.ed.asu.edu/volume1/number4/index.html>, and Fetterman (1998d), discussing the topic of learning with and about technology in *Meridian*, a middle school computer technology–oriented on-line journal at <http://www.ncsu.edu/meridian/jan98/index.html>. In addition, an on-line article about teaching in the virtual classroom (Fetterman, 1998e) can be found at <http://horizon.unc.edu/TS/cases/1998-08.asp>.

■ Conclusion

Empowerment evaluation has captured the attention and imagination of many evaluators throughout the world. Although characterized as a movement by some evaluators (Scriven, 1997a; Sechrest, 1997) because of its worldwide acceptance and the enthusiasm displayed by program participants, staff members, and empowerment evaluation coaches engaged in the process of improving programs and building capacity, empowerment evaluation is neither a movement nor a panacea. It is an approach that requires systematic and continual critical reflection and feedback, including the dissemination of this approach.

Empowerment evaluation has enjoyed rapid and widespread acceptance and use in part as a result of its link to the Internet. The Internet's capacity to disseminate information about empowerment evaluation in nanoseconds and on a global scale contributed substantially to this rapid dissemination of ideas. The synergistic relationship between empowerment evaluation and the Internet offers a model for others as they develop and refine their own approaches to evaluation. The Internet is unrivaled as a mechanism for the distribution of new ideas (particularly given the limited expense associated with the endeavor). The worldwide response to empowerment evaluation illustrates the strength and value arising from the marriages of new ideas and new technology.

The concluding chapter builds on the notion of universality. However, instead of focusing on the dissemination tool, it highlights the universality of self-assessment, critically examining the strengths, limitations, and conditions of empowerment evaluation.

CONCLUSION

Concluding by Speaking One's Truth About the Strengths, Limitations, and Conditions of Empowerment Evaluation

In times of universal deceit, telling the truth is a revolutionary act.

—*George Orwell*

Truth is what stands the test of experience.

—*Albert Einstein*

The fundamental strength of empowerment evaluation is its simplicity and universality in principle. It basically involves three steps: (a) mission, (b) taking stock, and (c) planning for the future. Progress toward specified goals are monitored using credible documentation as part of the normal planning and management of the program, which is a means of institutionalizing and internalizing evaluation.

141

Empowerment evaluation is characterized by its positive, constructive approach to life. However, it is not a naïve view. Positive and negative, including profoundly paralyzing, life experiences inform empowerment evaluation practice. Although most of the examples presented in this discussion focus on the positive, a brief example highlights the universal power of self-evaluation on a personal level from a less positive perspective in life. This example also highlights the significance of making a conscious, informed commitment to social change in spite, if not because of, the problems that plague humanity.[1]

Everyone has experienced deep, wrenching personal pain in their lives. They may have experienced a death in their family, marital infidelity, or betrayal in the workplace. I often ask workshop participants to get in touch with that pain, to feel it again for a moment, to remember it. I remind them that it was probably the most disempowering moment in their lives. I ask them how they dug themselves out of that emotional pit. The answer: evaluation. We assessed the situation—what happened, why it happened, what our role was in the situation, what others did or did not do—evaluating both the processes and outcomes in the situation. Then we took an inventory of our resources and liabilities, set goals, and specified and implemented strategies to accomplish those goals. We acted on our plans and monitored our relative success with each effort to regain our self-confidence and build toward the future.

I use this example because it reminds us that many of the program participants with whom we work live this pain everyday with no hope of escaping from the emotional paralysis associated with it. Their problems are typically complex, overlapping, and emotionally traumatic. A reminder of our own pain helps us rekindle a sensitivity and empathy for those who are still in the whirlwind, fearful, paralyzed, and often self-destructive. People are fundamentally responsible for their actions and should be held accountable for them; however, program staff members and participants do not always come through or live up to their commitments in a program or self-evaluation. An appreciation for their circumstances and pain enable an evaluation coach to accept the broken promises and still move forward.

This example also highlights the universality of self-assessment. We evaluate our own programs and practices every day. Evaluation is used to shop for goods and services, soul mates, friends, and a variety of social and educational programs. It is also used for personal and professional growth. Evaluation is a basic function of our existence. However, for it to be useful it must be honest. It is important to speak one's truth in an evaluation in order to reach one's goals and dreams. In this spirit, this book concludes with a brief review of the strengths, limitations, and conditions of empowerment.

■ Strengths

People represent empowerment evaluations greatest strength and weakness. The spirit of human beings in the pursuit of self- and program improvement is enormous and should not be underestimated. People can literally move mountains. Everyone brings special natural or cultivated talents to the table in an empowerment evaluation. The task is to identify and harness those talents. A few of the strengths of empowerment evaluation that help to bring many of these talents to the table include a collaborative process, emphasis on using evaluative data to inform decision making, and capacity building.

One of the most powerful strengths of empowerment evaluation is its ability to pull people together toward the common good. The collaborative process is democratic and inviting. It emphasizes inclusion, rather than exclusion. Joy Moreton (personal communication, 1998), the director of an empowerment evaluation project at Cambridge College, stated it simply: "The process works." Cambridge College faculty, staff members, and students are conducting a comprehensive empowerment evaluation across their institution. Her team participates in many of the long group meetings and activities requiring dialogue and consultation. Although logistically and at times interpersonally difficult, she has found that these collaborative consultations with various populations and departments within the institution are effective in pulling people together toward common, constructive goals and solutions.

Another strength of empowerment evaluation is its ability to use data to inform decision making. Rita O'Sullivan and Anne D'Agostino's (1998) collaborative work to promote evaluation with community-based programs for young children and their families highlights the strength of empowerment evaluation to dramatically alter the use of data to inform program operations and decision making. Their research documents the shift from data-free evaluation efforts of many of these programs, before engaging in collaborative and empowering evaluation activities,[2] to "some data-supported" and "mostly data-supported" efforts in one year of a multiagency collaborative empowerment evaluation engagement.

Debbie Zorn, M. Lynne Smith, and Imelda Castaneda's (1998) school-to-work evaluation efforts also highlight this strength of empowerment evaluation. They describe their role as "promoting local data-based decision making for schools' continuous improvement" (p. 1). Their aim is to help schools learn to use data to drive "their own self-determined improvement process" (p. 1).

Capacity building is another important strength associated with empowerment evaluation. Lynn Usher's Annie E. Casey Foundation–sponsored evaluative efforts in the area of family foster care exemplifies this strength. According to Usher (1996), "The first step in building a capacity for self-evaluation is to overcome skepticism that data actually can be useful" (p. 6). In many cases, new structures and processes for handling information are required to overcome data overload and consequent skepticism about the utility of data for decision making. A few of the tools used by Usher and others to build capacity across the state include the use of longitudinal data to determine the length of stay in out-of-home care for children; Geographic Information System software to enable social service providers to manipulate and display geographic information, such as placements; and statistical projections based on existing data residing in agencies' administrative files. These tools have been used to build capacity and enable providers to enhance their effectiveness.

There are many other strengths associated with empowerment evaluation, ranging from the democratic nature of the enterprise, which helps to provide a group self-check on major decisions, to the learning-community culture it can establish in an organization or program. However, there are also many limitations associated with the approach that merit discussion.

■ Limitations

Empowerment evaluation depends on people. Just as people can be empowerment evaluation's greatest asset, they can be a significant limitation. Groups have various skills. Organizational, analytical, and interpersonal skills are not always equally divided across programs or groups. Hostile, uncooperative groups, with a poor combination of skills, add a tremendous degree of difficulty to an empowerment evaluation project. In addition, the most skilled individuals often leave a program. Turnover is one of the most common and difficult problems associated with an ongoing, long-term effort such as empowerment evaluation. A charismatic, well-trained, conscientious, and well-liked program staff person or program participant is invaluable in sustaining a self-evaluative effort. Even though empowerment evaluation is a group activity, it is dependent on motivated and conscientious people. When they leave, a significant part of the evaluative momentum and energy can be lost as well. Additional limitations that merit discussion include the purpose of the evaluation and exploitation.

The value or strength of empowerment evaluation is directly linked to the purpose of the evaluation. Chelimsky (1997) discusses three different purposes of evaluation: (a) development, (b) accountability, and (c) knowledge, as noted in Chapter 8. Empowerment evaluation is strongest in the area of development—helping newly emerging or configured programs develop into mature sustainable entities. Empowerment evaluation makes a significant contribution to internal accountability, but has serious limitations in the area of external accountability. A bank analogy, often used to highlight the complementarity of internal and external evaluation, is also useful in discussing the strengths and limitations of empowerment evaluation in this area: Customer service might be improved if bank officers and tellers participated in an empowerment evaluation, listening to customer concerns about what they were looking for in terms of service, courtesy, and convenience; however, customers would also want an external evaluation or audit to make sure their money is being accounted for properly. An external audit or assessment would be more appropriate if the purpose of the evaluation was external accountability.

Another potential limitation or problem associated with empowerment evaluation is exploitation. Some sponsors believe empowerment evaluation is free. Nothing is free; empowerment evaluation takes time and requires resources. Generally, the largest effort is front-loaded and diminishes over time. However, empowerment evaluation coaches, program staff members, and participants should be compensated for their time and effort. Compensation may be in many forms, such as salaried support for specific coaching activities, as well as transcription and complex data collection and analysis efforts. Other forms of support may include computer equipment to facilitate electronic communication, database software to facilitate analysis, and supplies. In some cases, program staff members and participants should be compensated for part of the time they contribute to the evaluation. However, everyone should make some contribution as a good citizen in the program. (This will depend on the norm of the group or organization, availability of resources, and the time commitment required.)

There are many other potential limitations associated with the approach, including the fact that it can be extremely critical and bruise egos; that the degree of evaluative sophistication is dependent on the talents of program staff members, participants, and the evaluation coach; that it takes more time than most traditional evaluations because part of the effort must be devoted to team- and trust-building; and that sustainability is dependent on the degree to which the group is successful in institutionalizing evaluation. Each of these strengths and limitations are enhanced or exasperated by the conditions in which the program is operating.

■ Conditions

The best conditions for an empowerment evaluation are open and receptive arms, inviting the evaluation. Programs committed to inclusive, democratic, and self-critical engagements can make the most out of an empowerment evaluation. In other words, programs already operating in an empowerment or self-determined mode represent the best match for this approach. The worst conditions for this approach are found in dictatorial, dishonest, and distrusting environments. These environments might need this approach the most, but greater gains will be made in environments conducive to this evaluative style and approach. Conditions need not be perfect to conduct an empowerment evaluation. In some cases, it is more appropriate to apply empowerment evaluation concepts and techniques, instead of a full-blown empowerment evaluation. A program may request an empowerment evaluation without fully understanding what it entails. In addition, even informed clients need to shift from what they have experienced in the past to a new way of conducting evaluation—from within. The loss of control can be distressing for many managers and directors. In addition, program staff members and participants are busy and socialized in traditional roles as well. They typically will ask empowerment evaluation coaches to do the evaluation for them, even after inviting them to facilitate the effort. Coaches need to provide assistance on many levels, but they also have to remember to help program staff members and participants take charge of their own lives and the evaluation effort, fostering independence instead of dependency.

Time can be a limitation of the approach when there is little to spare. However, it is also a necessary condition in empowerment evaluation. This approach can take longer than a traditional evaluation because time is needed to build a collaborative, to build trust, and to set up new structures for operating across traditional boundaries. In addition, group work is initially time-consuming as people learn more about each other's strengths and weaknesses. This diminishes over time; however, it is an important factor to consider at the onset of an empowerment evaluation.

■ Conclusion: A Contextual Comment

Speaking one's truth is not always pleasant, but it is necessary to improve practice. This brief discussion about strengths, limitations, and conditions was presented with that belief and value commitment in mind. Empowerment evaluation has made a significant contribution to people and programs. However, there is still much to learn. An open dialogue about this approach in practice will only enhance its effectiveness and applicability. A simple exercise of this nature also provides empowerment evaluators with another opportunity to "walk their talk."

Empowerment evaluation has touched the hearts of many evaluators. It has generated tremendous debate and discussion in the field. This debate, which involves some of the most prominent colleagues in the field and appears in the evaluation field's primary journals, is symbolic of empowerment evaluation's impact.[3] As I reflect on this phenomenon, I can only speculate that the attention this approach is receiving is in part a function of both the utility of empowerment evaluation and the powerful contrast it creates with many traditional approaches. Empowerment evaluation has many purposes and many contributions to make to evaluation: as another tool in the evaluator's toolbox, as a vehicle to influence and improve traditional forms of evaluation (by inviting much greater involvement and participation by program participants in evaluation), and as a mechanism to clarify further and expand our understanding of what evaluation is.

I am appreciative (although somewhat surprised) by the level and type of discourse this approach has generated and the attention it has received. This kind of engagement can only improve and refine both empowerment evaluation and evaluation in general.

Empowerment evaluation is evolving. Its intent represents a shift from the narrow focus on merit and worth alone to a commitment to self-determination and capacity building. This shift is much like the emerging shift in medicine from a focus on disease to a focus on wellness. These are not clever word games. As Patton (1997a) points out, words shape meaning; they shape how we think about what we are doing and thus shape action.

Empowerment evaluation is appealing to evaluators committed to democratic forms of participation and decision making, to building capacity, to fostering independence and self-determination, and to cultivating a community of learners. Empowerment evaluators believe what House (1993) has stated so boldly, that evaluation "was invented to solve social problems" (p. 11). It may not be appropriate for evaluators who value the role of the external, distant expert above group interaction and participation. Empowerment evaluation is a group effort. It captures the imagination of evaluators and program participants who are committed to promoting responsible social change.

Empowerment evaluation has already helped to clarify how evaluators define evaluation, regardless of their place in the evaluation continuum. It has influenced traditional forms of evaluation and helped to distinguish similar but different approaches, such as participatory and collaborative forms of evaluation. I did not anticipate either the flurry of excitement or the stormy seas resulting from the introduction of this approach. In an echo of Prospero's blessing to Miranda in *The Tempest*, this experience has brought both calm seas and auspicious gales. I am deeply appreciative of my colleagues, both for and against this approach, who have taken the time to engage in this important dialogue.

■ Notes

1. Evaluators who adopt an empowerment evaluation approach with a naïve and utopian perspective are often disillusioned and retreat to traditional approaches. Evaluators with an insight into humanity at its lowest typically have more tolerance, patience, and endurance in this area.

2. O'Sullivan and D'Agostino have been extremely innovative using evaluation fairs to foster this sense of community and collaboration.

3. I appreciate and commend Blaine Worthen, a past editor of the *American Journal of Evaluation*, for orchestrating a professional exchange that helped us to reexamine the field of evaluation itself. He created an environment conducive to scholarly debate and inquiry, and thus facilitated both a discussion about empowerment evaluation as an approach and its role as a catalyst for a much larger discussion about the purpose(s) of evaluation.

Michael Patton shared his manuscript for the article "Toward Distinguishing Empowerment Evaluation and Placing It in a Larger Context" with me before publication, and I provided a long list of corrections and suggestions. He incorporated these, as deemed appropriate, to refine his argument in some instances and strengthen it in others. I am grateful to have had the opportunity to create a more focused exchange. This back-and-forth process has allowed us to focus our attention on crystallized and improved arguments, rather than on errors and omissions. This initial exchange has also set the stage for further dissemination of contrasting views from Michael Scriven and from me, in an effort to improve practice. In response to my request for permission to place his critique on the Collaborative, Participatory, and Empowerment Evaluation topical interest group home page

<http://www.stanford.edu/~davidf/empowermentevaluation.html>

Scriven responded, "Congratulations, this is in the best interests of science and evaluation." Immediately afterward, he offered to cross-link my response to the Internet homepage he is developing. I think our prepublication exchanges and our commitment to open debate and sharing of information provide a model that we should work to maintain, refine, and improve in our scholastic community.

Patton's and Scriven's comments provide valuable contributions to the development of empowerment evaluation. Their discussions should be mined for every ounce of insight to build and refine this approach. Embracing critique is in the true spirit of a self-reflective and growing evaluative community of learners.

REFERENCES

Altman, D. (1997). [Review of the book *Empowerment evaluation: Knowledge and tools for self-assessment and accountability*]. *Community Psychologist, 30*(4), 16–17. Available on-line at <http://www.stanford.edu/~davidf/altmanbkreview.html>.

American Evaluation Association Task Force on Guiding Principles for Evaluators. (1995). Guiding Principles for Evaluators. In W. R. Shadish, D. L. Newman, M. A. Scheirer, and C. Wye (Eds.), *Guiding principles for evaluators* (New Directions for Program Evaluation, Vol. 66, pp. 19–26). San Francisco: Jossey-Bass.

Andrews, A. (1996). Realizing participant empowerment in the evaluation of non-profit women's services organizations: Notes from the front line. In D. M. Fetterman, S. Kaftarian, and A. Wandersman (Eds.), *Empowerment evaluation: Knowledge and tools for self-assessment and accountability*. Thousand Oaks, CA: Sage.

Argyris, C., and Schon, D. (1978). *Organizational learning: A theory of action*. London: Perspective.

Ayers, T. D. (1987). Stakeholders as partners in evaluation: A stakeholder-collaborative approach. *Evaluation and Program Planning, 10*, 263–271.

Bandura, A. (1982). Self-efficacy mechanism in human agency. *American Psychologist, 37*, 122–147.

Berk, R., and Rossi, P. H. (1976). Doing good or worse: Evaluation research politically re-examined. *Social Problems, 23*(3), 337–349.

Bickman, L. (1987). *Using program theory in evaluation* (New Directions for Program Evaluation, Vol. 33). San Francisco: Jossey-Bass.

Brown, J. (1997). [Review of the book *Empowerment evaluation: Knowledge and tools for self-assessment and accountability*]. *Health Education and Behavior, 24*(3), 388–391. Available on-line at <http://www.stanford.edu/~davidf/brown.html>.

Brunner, I., and Guzman, A. (1989). Participatory evaluation: A tool to assess projects and empower people. In R. F. Connor and M. H. Hendricks (Eds.), *International innovations in evaluation methodology* (New Directions for Program Evaluation, Vol. 42, pp. 9–17). San Francisco: Jossey-Bass.

Bryk, A. (Ed.). (1983). *Stakeholder-based evaluation* (New Directions for Program Evaluation, Vol. 17). San Francisco: Jossey-Bass.

Burbules, N. C., and Bruce, B. C. (1995). This is not a paper. *Educational Researcher,* 24(8), 12–18.

Butterfoss, F. D., Goodman, R. M., Wandersman, A., Valois, R. F., and Chinman, M. J. (1996). The plan quality index: An empowerment evaluation tool for measuring and improving the quality of plans. In D. M. Fetterman, S. Kaftarian, and A. Wandersman (Eds.), *Empowerment evaluation: Knowledge and tools for self-assessment and accountability* (pp. 304–331). Thousand Oaks, CA: Sage.

Campbell, D. T. (1971). *Methods for the experimenting society.* Paper presented at the annual meeting of the American Psychological Association, Washington, DC.

Campbell, D. T. (1974). Degrees of Freedom and the case study. In T. D. Cook and C. S. Reichardt (Eds.), *Qualitative and quantitative methods in evaluation research* (pp. 49-67). Thousand Oaks, CA: Sage.

Chelimsky, E. (1997). The coming transformations in evaluation. In E. Chelimsky and W. Shadish (Eds.), *Evaluation for the 21st century: A handbook* (pp. 1–26). Thousand Oaks, CA: Sage.

Chelimsky, E., and Shadish, W. (Eds.). (1997). *Evaluation for the 21st century: A handbook.* Thousand Oaks, CA: Sage.

Chen, H. (1990). Issues in constructing program theory. In L. Bickman (Ed.), *Advances in program theory* (New Directions for Program Evaluation, Vol. 47, pp. 7–18). San Francisco: Jossey-Bass.

Choudhary, A., and Tandon, R. (1988). *Participatory evaluation.* New Delhi, India: Society for Participatory Research in Asia.

Connell, J. P., Kubisch, A. C., Schorr, L. B., and Weiss, C. H. (Eds.). (1995). *New approaches to evaluating community initiatives: Concepts, methods, and contexts.* Washington, DC: The Aspen Institute.

Conrad, K. J. (1994). *Critically evaluating the role of experiments* (New Directions for Program Evaluation, Vol. 63). San Francisco: Jossey-Bass.

Cook, T., and Shadish, W. (1994). Social experiments: Some developments over the past fifteen years. *Annual Review of Psychology, 45,* 545–580.

Cousins, J. B. (1998, November). *Evaluator versus program practitioner perspectives in collaborative evaluation.* Paper presented at the annual meeting of the American Evaluation Association, Chicago, IL.

Cousins, J. B., Donohue, J. J., and Bloom, G. A. (1996). Collaborative evaluation in North America: Evaluators' self-reported opinions, practices and consequences. *Evaluation Practice, 17*(3), 207–226.

Cousins, J. B., and Earl, L. M. (1992). The case for participatory evaluation. *Educational Evaluation and Policy Analysis, 14*(4), 397–418.

Cousins, J. B., and Earl, L. M. (Eds.). (1995). *Participatory evaluation in education: Studies of evaluation use and organizational learning.* London: Falmer.

Cronbach, L. J. (1980). *Toward reform of program evaluation.* San Francisco: Jossey-Bass.

Csikszentmihalyi, M. (1990). *Creativity: Flow and the psychology of discovery and invention.* New York: Harper & Row.

Dugan, M. (1996). Participatory and empowerment evaluation: Lessons learned in training and technical assistance. In D. M. Fetterman, S. Kaftarian, and A. Wandersman (Eds.), *Empowerment evaluation: Knowledge and tools for self-assessment and accountability* (pp. 227–303). Thousand Oaks, CA: Sage.

Dunst, C. J., Trivette, C. M., and LaPointe, N. (1992). Toward clarification of the meaning and key elements of empowerment. *Family Science Review, 5*(1–2), 111–130.

Fawcett, S., Paine-Andrews, A., Francisco, V. T., Schultz, J. A., Richter, K. P., Lewis, R. K., Harris, K. J., Williams, E. L., Berkley, J. Y., Lopez, C. M., and Fisher, J. L. (1996). Empowering community health initiatives through evaluation. In D. M. Fetterman, S. Kaftarian, and A. Wandersman (Eds.), *Empowerment evaluation: Knowledge and tools for self-assessment and accountability* (pp. 161–187). Thousand Oaks, CA: Sage.

Fetterman, D. M. (1982). Ibsen's baths: Reactivity and insensitivity (A misapplication of the treatment-control design in a national evaluation). *Educational Evaluation and Policy Analysis, 4*(3), 261–279.

Fetterman, D. M. (1989). *Ethnography: Step by step.* Thousand Oaks, CA: Sage.

Fetterman, D. M. (1993a, October 3). Confronting a culture of violence: South Africa nears a critical juncture. *San Jose Mercury*, pp. C1, C4.

Fetterman, D. M. (1993b). Ethnography and policy: Translating knowledge into action. In D. M. Fetterman (Ed.), *Speaking the language of power: Communication, collaboration, and advocacy* (pp. 170–171). London: Falmer.

Fetterman, D. M. (1993c). Theme for the 1993 annual meeting: Empowerment evaluation. *Evaluation Practice, 14*(1), 115–117.

Fetterman, D. M. (1994a). Empowerment evaluation [American Evaluation Association presidential address]. *Evaluation Practice, 15*(1), 1–15.

Fetterman, D. M. (1994b). Steps of empowerment evaluation: From California to Cape Town. *Evaluation and Program Planning, 17*(3), 305–313.

Fetterman, D. M. (1995). [Response to D. Stufflebeam, Empowerment evaluation, objectivist evaluation, and evaluation standards: Where the future of evaluation should not go and where it needs to go.] *Evaluation Practice, 16*(2), 179–199.

Fetterman, D. M. (1995). In Response to Dr. Daniel Stufflebeam's: "Empowerment Evaluation, Objectivist Evaluation, and Evaluation Standards: Where the Future of Evaluation Should Not Go and Where It Needs to Go," *Evaluation Practice,* June 1995, 16(2): 179-199. <http://www.stanford.edu/~davidf/stufflebeamresponse.html>.

Fetterman, D. M. (1996a). Empowerment evaluation: An introduction to theory and practice. In D. M. Fetterman, S. Kaftarian, and A. Wandersman (Eds.), *Empowerment evaluation: Knowledge and tools for self-assessment and accountability* (pp. 13–14). Thousand Oaks, CA: Sage.

Fetterman, D. M. (1996b). Ethnography in the virtual classroom. *Practicing Anthropology, 18*(3), 2, 36–39.

Fetterman, D. M. (1996c). Videoconferencing: Enhancing communication on the Internet. *Educational Researcher, 25*(4), 23–27.

Fetterman, D. M. (1997a). Empowerment evaluation: A response to Patton and Scriven. *Evaluation Practice, 18*(3), 253–266. Available on-line at <http://www.stanford.edu/~davidf/pattonscriven.html>.

Fetterman, D. M. (1997b). [Response to L. Sechrest, review of *Empowerment evaluation: Knowledge and tools for self-assessment and accountability*]. *Environment and Behavior, 29*(3), 427–436. <http://www.stanford.edu/~davidf/fettermansechrest.html>.

Fetterman, D. M. (1998a). Empowerment evaluation and accreditation in higher education. In E. Chelimsky and W. Shadish (Eds.), *Evaluation for the 21st century: A handbook* (pp. 381–395). Thousand Oaks, CA: Sage.

Fetterman, D. M. (1998b). Empowerment evaluation and the Internet: A synergistic relationship. *Current Issues in Education [On-line], 1*(4). Available on-line at <http://cie.ed.asu.edu/volume1/number4/index.html>.

Fetterman, D. M. (1998c). *Ethnography: Step by step* (2nd ed.). Thousand Oaks, CA: Sage.

Fetterman, D. M. (1998d). Learning *with* and *about* technology: A middle school nature area. *Meridian, [On-line] 1*(1). Available on-line at <http://www.ncsu.edu/meridian/jan98>.

Fetterman, D. M. (1998e). Teaching in the virtual classroom at Stanford University. *Technology Source [On-line].* Available on-line at <http://horizon.unc.edu/TS/cases/1998-08.asp>.

Fetterman, D. M., and Haertel, E. H. (1990). A school-based evaluation model for accelerating the education of students at-risk. Clearinghouse on Urban Education, ERIC, ED 313 495.

Fetterman, D. M., Kaftarian, S., and Wandersman, A. (Eds.). (1996). *Empowerment evaluation: Knowledge and tools for self-assessment and accountability.* Thousand Oaks, CA: Sage.

Fournier, D. M. (Ed.). (1995). *Reasoning in evaluation: Inferential links and leaps* (New Directions for Evaluation, Vol. 68). San Francisco, CA: Jossey-Bass.

Gomez, C. A., and Goldstein, E. (1996). The HIV Prevention evaluation initiative: a model for collaborative and empowerment evaluation. In D. M. Fetterman, S. Kaftarian, and A. Wandersman (Eds.), *Empowerment evaluation: Knowledge and tools for self-assessment and accountability* (pp. 100–122). Thousand Oaks, CA: Sage.

Greene, J. C. (1988). Stakeholder participation and utilization in program evaluation. *Evaluation Review, 12*(2), 91–116.

Greene, J. C. (1997). Evaluation as advocacy. *Evaluation Practice, 18*(1), 25–35.

Grills, C. N., Bass, K., Brown, D. L., and Akers, A. (1996). Empowerment evaluation: Building upon a tradition of activism in the African American community. In D. M. Fetterman, S. Kaftarian, and A. Wandersman (Eds.), *Empowerment evaluation: Knowledge and tools for self-assessment and accountability* (pp. 123–140). Thousand Oaks, CA: Sage.

Habermas, J. (1984). *The theory of communicative action* (Vol. 1). Boston, MA: Beacon.

Hess, F. (1993). Testifying on the Hill: Using ethnographic data to shape public policy. In D. M. Fetterman (Ed.), *Speaking the language of power: Communication, collaboration, and advocacy* (pp. 38–49). London: Falmer.

Hopper, K. (1993). On keeping an edge: Translating ethnographic findings and putting them to use: NYC's homeless policy. In D. M. Fetterman (Ed.), *Speaking the language of power: Communication, collaboration, and advocacy* (pp. 19–37). London: Falmer.

House, E. R. (1980). *Evaluating with validity.* Beverly Hills, CA: Sage.

House, E. R. (1993). *Professional evaluation.* Thousand Oaks, CA: Sage.

House, E. R. (1998). The issue of advocacy in evaluations. *American Journal of Evaluation, 19*(2), 233–236.

House, E. R., and Howe, K. R. (in press). *Values in evaluation and social research.* Thousand Oaks, CA: Sage.

Joint Committee on Standards for Educational Evaluation. (1994). *The program evaluation standards.* Thousand Oaks, CA: Sage. Available on-line at <http://www.eval.org/EvaluationDocuments/progeval.html>.

Keller, J. (1996). Empowerment evaluation and safe government. Moving from resistance to adoption. In D. Fetterman, S. Kaftarian, & A. Wandersman (Eds.), *Empowerment evalauation: Knowledge and tools for self-assessment and accountability.* Thousand Oaks, CA: Sage.

King, J. A. (1998). Making sense of participatory evaluation practice. In E. Whitmore (Ed.), *Understanding and practicing participatory evaluation* (New Directions for Evaluation, Vol. 80, pp. 57–68). San Francisco: Jossey-Bass.

Kretzmann, J., and McKnight, J. (1990). *Mapping community capacity* [On-line document]. Chicago: Northwestern University, Center for Urban Affairs and Policy Research. Available on-line at <http://www.nwu.edu/IPR/publications/mcc.html>.

Kretzmann, J., McKnight, J., and Sheehan, G. (1997). *A guide to capacity inventories: Mobilizing the community skills of local residents.* Chicago: Northwestern University, Institute for Policy Research, Northwestern University. Available on-line at <http://www.nwu.edu/IPR/publications/capinv.html>.

Levin, H. M. (1996). Empowerment evaluation and accelerated schools. In D. M. Fetterman, S. Kaftarian, and A. Wandersman (Eds.), *Empowerment evaluation: Knowledge and tools for self-assessment and accountability* (pp. 49–64). Thousand Oaks, CA: Sage.

Linney, J. A., and Wandersman, A. (1991). *Prevention Plus III: Assessing alcohol and other drug prevention programs at the school and community level: A four-step guide to useful program assessment.* Rockville, MD: U.S. Department of Health and Human Services, Office of Substance Abuse Prevention.

Linney, J. A., and Wandersman, A. (1996). Empowering community groups with evaluation skills: The Prevention Plus III model. In D. M. Fetterman, S. Kaftarian, and A. Wandersman (Eds.), *Empowerment evaluation: Knowledge and tools for self-assessment and accountability* (pp. 259–276). Thousand Oaks, CA: Sage.

Mayer, S. E. (1996). Building community capacity with evaluation activities that empower. In D. M. Fetterman, S. Kaftarian, and A. Wandersman (Eds.), *Empowerment evaluation: Knowledge and tools for self-assessment and accountability* (pp. 332–375). Thousand Oaks, CA: Sage.

McClintock, C. (1990). Administrators as applied theorists. In L. Bickman (Ed.), *Advances in program theory* (New Directions for Program Evaluation, Vol. 47, pp. 19–33). San Francisco: Jossey-Bass.

Mezirow, J. (1978). *Education for perspective transformation: Women's re-entry programs in community settings.* New York: Columbia University Teachers College, Center for Adult Education.

Millett, R. (1996). Empowerment evaluation and the W. K. Kellogg Foundation. In D. M. Fetterman, S. Kaftarian, and A. Wandersman (Eds.), *Empowerment evaluation: Knowledge and tools for self-assessment and accountability* (pp. 65–76). Thousand Oaks, CA: Sage.

Mills, C. (1959). *The sociological imagination.* New York: Oxford University Press.

Mithaug, D. E. (1991). *Self-determined kids: Raising satisfied and successful children.* New York: Macmillan.

Mithaug, D. E. (1993). *Self-regulation theory: How optimal adjustment maximizes gain.* New York: Praeger.

Moreton, J., and Pursley, L. (1998). *Cambridge College research and evaluation project* [Monograph]. Cambridge, MA: Cambridge College.

Oja, S. N., and Smulyan, L. (1989). *Collaborative action research.* London: Falmer.

O'Sullivan, R., and D'Agostino, A. (1998, November). *How collaborative approaches promote evaluation with community-based programs for young children and their families.* Paper presented at the annual meeting of the American Evaluation Association, Chicago, IL.

Papineau, D., and Kiely, M. C. (1994). Participatory evaluation: Empowering stakeholders in a community economic development organization. *Community Psychologist, 27*(2), 56–57.

Parker, L., and Langley, B. (1993). Protocol and policy-making systems in American Indian tribes. In D. M. Fetterman (Ed.), *Speaking the language of power: Communication, collaboration, and advocacy* (pp. 70–75). London: Falmer.

Partlett, M., and Hamilton, D. (1976). Evaluation as illumination: A new approach to the study of innovatory programmes. In D. Hamilton (Ed.), *Beyond the numbers game* (pp. 6-22). London: Macmillan.

Patton, M. Q. (1989). A context and boundaries for theory-driven approach to validity. *Evaluation and Program Planning, 12*, 375–377.

Patton, M. Q. (1994). Developmental evaluation. *Evaluation Practice, 15*(3), 311–320.

Patton, M. Q. (1997a). Toward distinguishing empowerment evaluation and placing it in a larger context. *Evaluation Practice, 18*(2), 147–163. Available on-line at <http://www.stanford.edu/~davidf/patton.html>.

Patton, M. Q. (1997b). *Utilization-focused evaluation: The new century text.* (3rd ed.). Thousand Oaks, CA: Sage.

Porteous, N. L., Sheldrick, B. J., and Stewart, P. J. (1997). *Program evaluation tool kit: A blueprint for public health management* [Monograph]. Ottawa: Ottawa-Carleton Health Department.

Preskill, H. (1994). Evaluation's role in enhancing organizational learning. *Evaluation and Program Planning, 17*(3), 291–297.

Preskill, H., and Caracelli, V. (1997). Current and developing conceptions of use: Evaluation use TIG survey results. *Evaluation Practice, 18*(3), 209–225.

Rappaport, J. (1987) Terms of empowerment/Exemplars of prevention: Toward a theory for community psychology. *American Journal of Community Psychology, 15*, 121–148.

Reason, P. (Ed.). (1988). *Human inquiry in action: Developments in new paradigm research.* Newbury Park, CA: Sage.

Sanders, J. R., Barley, Z. A., and Jenness, M. R. (1990). *Annual report: Cluster evaluation in science education.* Unpublished report.

Scriven, M. (1967). The methodology of evaluation. In R. E. Stake (Ed.), *Curriculum evaluation* (AERA Monograph Series on Curriculum Evaluation, Vol. 1). Chicago: Rand McNally.

Scriven, M. (1991). *Evaluation thesaurus* (4th ed.). Thousand Oaks, CA: Sage.

Scriven, M. (1993). *Hard-won lessons in evaluation* (New Directions for Program Evaluation, Vol. 58). San Francisco: Jossey-Bass.

Scriven, M. (1997a). Empowerment evaluation examined. *Evaluation Practice, 18*(2), 165–175. Available on-line at <http://www.stanford.edu/~davidf/scriven.html>.

Scriven, M. (1997b). Truth and objectivity in evaluation. In E. Chelimsky. and W. Shadish (Eds.), *Evaluation for the 21st century: A handbook* (pp. 477–500). Thousand Oaks, CA: Sage.

Sechrest, L. (1997). [Review of the book *Empowerment evaluation: Knowledge and tools for self-assessment and accountability*]. *Environment and Behavior, 29*(3), 422–426. Available on-line at <http://www.stanford.edu/~davidf/sechrest. html>.

Shadish, W. R. (1998). Evaluation theory is who we are. *American Journal of Evaluation, 19*(1), 1–19.

Shapiro, J. P. (1988). Participatory evaluation: Toward a transformation of assessment for women's studies programs and projects. *Educational Evaluation and Policy Analysis, 10*(3), 191–199.

Soffer, E. (1995). The principal as action researcher: A study of disciplinary practice. In S. E. Noffke and R. B. Stevenson (Eds.), *Educational action research: Becoming practically critical* (pp. 115-126). New York: Teachers College Press.

Stake, R. E. (1995). *The art of case study research.* Thousand Oaks, CA: Sage.

Stanford University and American Institutes for Research. (1992). A design for systematic support for accelerated schools: In response to the New American Schools Development Corporation RFP for designs for a new generation of American schools. Palo Alto, CA: Author.

Stevenson, J. F., Mitchell, R. E., and Florin, P. (1996). Evaluation and self-direction in community prevention coalitions. In D. M. Fetterman, S. Kaftarian, and A. Wandersman (Eds.). *Empowerment evaluation: Knowledge and tools for self-assessment and accountability* (pp. 208–233). Thousand Oaks, CA: Sage.

Stufflebeam, D. L. (1994). Empowerment evaluation, objectivist evaluation, and evaluation standards: Where the future of evaluation should not go and where it needs to go. *Evaluation Practice, 15*(3), 321–338.

Stull, D., and Schensul, J. (1987). *Collaborative research and social change: Applied anthropology in action.* Boulder, CO: Westview.

Tax, S. (1958). The fox project. *Human Organization, 17,* 17–19.

Timar, T. (1994). Federal educational policy and practice: Building organizational capacity through Chapter 1. *Educational Evaluation and Policy Analysis, 16*(1), 51–66.

Torres, R. T., Preskill, H. S., and Piontek, M. E. (1996). *Evaluation strategies for communicating and reporting: Enhancing learning in organizations.* Thousand Oaks, CA: Sage.

U.S. Department of Education. (1997). *Making information work for you: A guide for collecting good information and using it to improve comprehensive strategies for children, families, and communities.* Washington, DC: Policy Studies Associates and SRI International.

U.S. Department of Justice. (1995). *Community self-evaluation workbook.* Washington, DC: Office of Juvenile Justice and Delinquency Prevention.

United Way of America. (1996a). *Focusing on program outcomes: A guide for United Ways* [Monograph]. Alexandria, VA: Author.

United Way of America. (1996b). *Measuring program outcomes: A practical approach* [Monograph]. Alexandria, VA: Author.

Usher, C. L. (1995). Improving evaluability through self-evaluation. *Evaluation Practice, 16*(1), 59–68.

Usher, C. L. (1996). *The need for self-evaluation: Using data to guide policy and practice.* Baltimore, MD: The Annie E. Casey Foundation.

Vanderplaat, M. (1995). Beyond technique: issues in evaluating for empowerment. *Evaluation, 1*(1), 81–96.

Vanderplaat, M. (1997). Emancipatory politics, critical evaluation, and government policy. *Canadian Journal of Program Evaluation, 12*(2), 143–162.

W. K. Kellogg Foundation. (1992). *Transitions.* Battle Creek, MI: Author.

W. K. Kellogg Foundation. (1999). *Empowerment evaluation and foundations: A matter of perspectives.* Battle Creek, MI: Author.

Wadsworth, Y. (1997). *Everyday evaluation on the run.* Sydney, Australia: Allen and Unwin.

Wandersman, A., Imm, P., Crusto, C., and Andra, M. (1999, November). *Results-oriented grant-making/Grant-implementation: Evaluation strategies for local foundation initiatives.* Paper presented at the annual meeting of the American Evaluation Association, Orlando, FL.

Weeks, M. R., and Schensul, J. J. (1993). Ethnographic research on AIDS risk behavior and the making of policy. In D. M. Fetterman (Ed.), *Speaking the language of power: Communication, collaboration, and advocacy* (pp. 50–69). London: Falmer.

Weiss, C. H. (1998). *Evaluation* (2nd ed.). Englewood Cliffs, NJ: Prentice Hall.

Whitmore, E. (1991). Evaluation and empowerment. It's the process that counts. *Empowerment and Family Support Networking Bulletin* (Cornell University Empowerment Project), *2*(2), 1-7.

Whitmore, E. (Ed.) (1998). *Understanding and practicing participatory evaluation* (New Directions for Evaluation, Vol. 80). San Francisco: Jossey-Bass.

Wholey, J. (Ed.). (1987). *Organizational excellence: Stimulating quality and communicating value*. Lexington, MA: Lexington Books.

Whyte, W. F. (Ed.). (1990). *Participatory action research*. Newbury Park, CA: Sage.

Wild, T. (1997). [Review of *Empowerment evaluation: Knowledge and tools for self-assessment and accountability*]. *Canadian Journal of Program Evaluation, 11*(2), 170–172. Available on-line at <http://www.stanford.edu/~davidf/wild.html>.

Yin, R. K., Kaftarian, S., and Jacobs, N. F. (1996). Empowerment evaluation and the federal and local levels: Dealing with quality. In D. M. Fetterman, S. Kaftarian, and A. Wandersman (Eds.), *Empowerment evaluation: Knowledge and tools for self-assessment and accountability* (pp. 188–207). Thousand Oaks, CA: Sage.

Yost, J. B. (1998, November). *Empowerment evaluation and results-oriented grantsmaking in foundations*. Paper presented at the annual meeting of the American Evaluation Association, Chicago, IL.

Zimmerman, K., and Erbstein, N. (1999). Youth empowerment evaluation. *Evaluation Exchange, 5*(1), 4.

Zimmerman, M. A. (in press). Empowerment theory: Psychological, organizational, and community levels of analysis. In J. Rappaport and E. Seldman (Eds.), *Handbook of community psychology* (pp. 2–45). New York: Plenum.

Zimmerman, M. A., Israel, B. A., Schulz, A., and Checkoway, B. (1992). Further explorations in empowerment theory: An empirical analysis of psychological empowerment. *American Journal of Community Psychology, 20*(6), 707–727.

Zimmerman, M. A., and Rappaport, J. (1988). Citizen participation, perceived control, and psychological empowerment. *American Journal of Community Psychology, 16*(5), 725–750.

Zorn, D., Smith, M. L., and Castaneda, I. R. (1998, November). *Transforming schools through evaluation: A dialogue on initiating a school-to-work reform transition*. Paper presented at the annual meeting of the American Evaluation Association, Chicago, IL.

NAME INDEX

SUBJECT INDEX

ABOUT
THE
AUTHOR

David M. Fetterman is a member of the faculty and the director of the MA Policy Analysis and Evaluation Program in the School of Education at Stanford University. He was formerly a professor and research director at the California Institute of Integral Studies; a principal research scientist at the American Institutes for Research; and a senior associate and project director at RMC Research Corporation. He received his Ph.D. from Stanford University in educational and medical anthropology. He has conducted fieldwork in both Israel and the United States. Dr. Fetterman works in the fields of educational evaluation, ethnography, policy analysis, and educational technology, and focuses on programs for dropouts and gifted and talented education. He is a past president of the American Evaluation Association and the American Anthropological Association's Council on Anthropology and Education, and has served as the program chair for each of these organizations.

Dr. Fetterman has also worked on the state, national, and international level in the field of gifted and talented education. He created and organized the first and second Gifted and Talented Education Conference at Stanford University and was appointed by the U.S. Department of Education to serve on a panel to select a national center for the gifted and talented. The center is now in operation, and he is a member of its Consultant Bank, currently advising the National Research Center on the Gifted and Talented. Fetterman is also a member of the Board of Trustees for the Nueva School, a progressive school for gifted and talented children.

He has conducted extensive multisite evaluation research on local, state, and national levels, primarily in urban settings, including conducting a 3-year national evaluation of drop-out programs for the Department of Education. He has also conducted evaluations of migrant, bilingual, environmental health and safety, hospital, library, teacher education, academic and administrative, and individuals with disabilities programs. In addition, he has consulted for a variety of federal agencies, foundations, corporations, and academic institutions, including the Department of Education, National Institute of Mental Health, the Centers for Disease Control, the U.S. Department of Agriculture, the W. K. Kellogg Foundation, the Rockefeller Foundation, the Walter S. Johnson Foundation, the Annie E. Casey Foundation, Syntex, the Independent Development Trust in South Africa, the Early Childhood Research Institute on Full Inclusion, and universities throughout the United States and Europe.

Dr. Fetterman was elected a fellow of the American Anthropological Association and the Society for Applied Anthropology. He has received both the Myrdal Award for Evaluation Practice and the Lazarsfeld Award for Evaluation Theory—the American Evaluation Association's highest honors; the George and Louise Spindler Award for outstanding contributions to educational anthropology as a scholar and practitioner; the Ethnographic Evaluation Award from the Council on Anthropology and Education; the President's Award from the Evaluation Research Society for contributions to ethnographic educational evaluation; the Washington Association of Practicing Anthropologists' Praxis Publication Award for translating knowledge into action; and one of the 1990 Mensa Education and Research Foundation Awards for Excellence for *Excellence and Equality: A Qualitatively Different Perspective on Gifted and Talented Education* and articles on gifted and talented education in *Educational Evaluation and Policy Analysis* and *Gifted Education International*.

Dr. Fetterman has taught on-line for over seven years in an on-line Ph.D. program and in classrooms at Stanford University, complementing face-to-face instruction. He writes about teaching on-line and video-conferencing on the Internet in journals ranging from *Educational Researcher* to *Practicing Anthropology*, and maintains an American Evaluation Association division listserv for collaborative, participatory, and empowerment evaluation. Dr. Fetterman was recently appointed to the American Educational Research Association's Telecommunications Committee, advising the association in this area.

Dr. Fetterman is the general editor for Garland/Taylor and Francis Publication's Studies in Education and Culture series. He has contributed to a variety of encyclopedias including the *International Encyclopedia of Education* and the *Encyclopedia of Human Intelligence*. He is also the author of *Empowerment Evaluation: Knowledge and Tools for Self-Assessment and Accountability; Speaking the Language of Power: Communication, Collaboration, and Advocacy; Ethnography: Step by Step; Qualitative Approaches to Evaluation in Education: The Silent Scientific Revolution; Excellence and Equality: A Qualitatively Different Perspective on Gifted and Talented Education; Educational Evaluation: Ethnography in Theory, Practice, and Politics;* and *Ethnography in Educational Evaluation.*